Secret Places of the Heart

EUTHA SCHOLL

TRILOGY

Trilogy Christian Publishers
A Wholly Owned Subsidary of Trinity Broadcasting Network
2442 Michelle Drive
Tustin, CA 92780

For information, address Trilogy Christian Publishing
Rights Department, 2442 Michelle Drive, Tustin, Ca 92780.
Trilogy Christian Publishing/ TBN and colophon are trademarks of Trinity Broadcasting Network.

For information about special discounts for bulk purchases, please contact Trilogy Christian Publishing.

Manufactured in the United States of America

10 9 8 7 6 5 4 3 2 1

Library of Congress Cataloging-in-Publication Data is available.

ISBN 978-1-64088-786-2 (Print Book)
ISBN 978-1-64088-787-9 (ebook)

*Behold you delight in truth in the
inward being. You've taught me
wisdom in the secret place of the heart.*

—Psalms 51:6 (ESV)

CONTENTS

FOREWORD

To everyone reading this book, it was written by someone who has been on the dark side of life; and by the grace of God, she has come through and is able to put into words the things that the Lord inspires her to write. I have known Eutha, the author of this book, all of her life. I am her aunt and have seen where she has been and where she is now. Every word written comes from the Word of God and from the bottom of her heart. She has been in the grips of Satan, but the power of the Lord and His Son, Jesus, have brought her out for this purpose—so others who are fighting, trying to find themselves, can know they are not alone. As long as they have Jesus, there is hope for tomorrow. It is her aim that all who read this book come to believe there is a higher power, and if we stay strong in the Word of God, we will see and be with the Lord. No matter what Satan puts in our path, again I have seen Eutha at her worst and now at her best—in love with the Word of God.

Lavanda Morrick

PREFACE

I have written this book out of my desire to draw closer to the Father. I would like to take you with me to touch the very edge of heaven to join me in the secret place into the very throne room of our Father. As God has spoken to my heart, "Thus saith the Lord. Write in a book all the words I have given you" (Jeremiah 30:2), my desire is to share them with you as I journey toward home that you may join with me on the wall as warriors of our Father. As we guard spiritually against the tide of evil that seeks to overcome our families, our cities, and, our nation, my prayer would be that you would journey with me as we seek the Father's heart.

CHAPTER 1

Whispers of Angel Wings

In the predawn, I hear Your Spirit whisper, "Come into your secret place with Me. Awaken, come, and hear. Open your spiritual ear. Listen to My Spirit in the silence with angel wings fluttering near. Awaken, wipe the sleep from your eyes. Hear Me as we enter the tabernacle of My Word."

CHAPTER 2

Angel Wings

Whispers of angel wings awaken me. At the sound of Your voice, they come to guard Your child. As the night turns into day, I welcome them. The Son of the Morning Star comes riding on His white horse slaying spirits of the underworld in His path with His Word as His sword. He gallops through our life, asking us to join Him in battle just a breath away. Again, the angel wings flutter. The ultimate battle has begun with the sound of the shofar (the ram's horn). He calls His people out of slumber into battle. "Do not tremble nor be afraid [of the violent upheavals to come]; Have I not long ago proclaimed it to you and declared it? And you are My witnesses. Is there a God besides Me? There is no other Rock; I know of none" (Isaiah 44:8, AMP). "The Lord of hosts is mustering an army for battle with the unity of Spirit I call them" (Isaiah 13:4, NRSV). "I am the first and the last there is no God beside Me. Listen now with an open [spiritual] ear" (Isaiah 44:14, ESV). Angel wings flutter around us like doves calling into the night. We hear them at the sound of the shofar. They cry out, "Holy, holy, holy is He who sits on the throne." Do not remember the former things; they are the past. Listen carefully as the angels hold their breath around the throne. "I'm about to do a new thing even now it springs forth. Will you not know of it?" (Acts 13:41, ESV). "The people whom I formed for Myself will make My praises known. Awaken My people for the time is short" (Isaiah 43:21, AMP).

CHAPTER 3

Whispers of the Word

I awaken in the night in the dawn before the sun arises to bring my worship to You. I invite You, Holy Spirit, into my day. You say the Word and the darkness turns to light. I hear the whispers of Your Spirit speaking to my heart. The beauty of Your Word this morning keeps me in awe of You. I lean into hear the message of Your Words. In the book of Isaiah 30:21 (AMP), it says, "Your ear shall hear a word saying this is the way walk ye in it. When you turn to the right or to the left in quietness and trust, He will be your strength."

"My strength comes from His Spirit within me" (Ephesians 3:16, AMP), indwelling my innermost being and personality.

CHAPTER 4

At the end of a weary week, we stretch our arms upward like a child who is tired, who sees her Father. Father, reach down and take our hands. Pull us up into Your throne room. As we cry, here I am to worship. Here I am to bow down, to say that You are my God. As we rest in Your Spirit, let the tiredness and the cares of the week fade away. We welcome Your presence, Lord. Let Your presence renews us. For tomorrow we must battle. But today we find rest in Your presence, hidden away in the secret place under the shadow of Your wings (Psalms 36:7, ESV). The children of mankind take refuge in the shadow of your wings (Psalms 91:15, ESV). He will cover you with His feathers. He will shelter you with His wings. His faithful promises are your armor and His protection.

CHAPTER 5

Building Bridges

Two brothers lived side by side, just a small creek between them. They got into an argument, and they no longer spoke to each other. One day a man came by the elder brother's house and asked, "Do you have any work that I could do?" The elder son said, "Yes, actually I would like you to build a wall high enough to keep my brother out. He's broke down the dam. Now we have a pond that is not crossable between us. I have to go away for a while but will give you the money to build the wall."

The elder brother was gone longer than he expected. But when he returned, the elderly man was gone. Instead of a wall, he had built a bridge across the water. In the distance, he could see his brother walk onto the far side of the bridge. At the middle of the bridge, the younger brother, when they met, put out his hand and said, "Thank you for building the bridge between us." Do you have someone in your life who've you built walls in your spirit against? Wall that says, "He started it! I won't be treated this way!"

The Holy Spirit wants to build a bridge to take down the walls. Are there people you need to repair your relationship with by extending a hand? Ask yourself, what about me and my part of the wall? The Spirit says, *Take down the walls in your life.* Ask yourself, was the wall built to keep others out or to fence yourself in? "Have mercy on me, O God, according to Your steadfast love; according to Your abundant mercy. Wash me thoroughly from my iniquity, and cleanse me from my sin" (Psalms 51:1–2, ESV). You delight in the inward being. You teach me wisdom in the secret place in my heart.

CHAPTER 6

Map for the Journey Home

When you have a special book or fine wine you treasure, you put it in a special place, proudly displaying it for all to see. A book signed by the author of the book is to be even more treasured. We have such a book—the Bible. Do we proudly display the Bible? Like Christopher Columbus's maps, the Bible is a map for our journey home. Do we study it relentlessly to stay our course? Do we research it to find our way so we do not get lost on this journey? Or do we put it on a shelf with the many other dry dusty maps of life relegated to just another obsolete map or book?

The Bible, the written Word of God, is awe-inspired by the Holy Spirit. "In the beginning was the Word, and the Word was with God. The Word was God" (John 1:1, ESV). It is signed by the author in the blood of His Son. As Christopher Columbus set sail for the new world, he did not know where his journey would take him. So it is with us our journey; it is unknown. Our future is uncertain. But we know this: "Every Word of God is tested and refined like silver" (Proverbs 30:5, AMP).

Our journey home is to heaven the great throne room of God. The Bible is our map. We must study it, pore over it, researching it. This is the very living, breathing Word of God. The only map we have for our journey home. "My eyes wake before the watches of the night. That I may meditate on your promises in your Word" (Psalms 119:47–48, NIV).

CHAPTER 7

A Layered Heart

A layered heart can be best described as "when your heart gets layered over by protectiveness because of tough life hits or tough ministry situations." We feel the need to protect ourselves. It's not a rebellious heart but a heart layered over with a protective finish like a refinished piece of furniture. What can happen? However, through this process, a person gets less sensitive to the hearts of others. We eventually even use this same veneer with God: "We say this close and no farther." We distance ourselves from others in order not to get hurt. A finish of protectiveness that shuts others out also shuts us in. Your inner world matters. You cannot solve everything with your head. We cannot solve the surrounding conflict until we deal with the conflict in us.

God looks upon the heart, not the outward circumstances. He is looking for a humble, open heart—a heart that is pliable, teachable. Without the Holy Spirit in our lives, the veneer hardens increasingly each time we take a hit, whether it be emotional or physical. Bill Hybels said, "Open your Spiritual ears to the council, Your Father wants to communicate to you today."

Let the Holy Spirit strip away the veneer, the layers of protection, around your heart. Learn to build bridges with other people, not walls.

CHAPTER 8

Personal Integrity versus Freedom

In 2 Kings 22:16 (ESV), Josiah found a book of the law in the house of the Lord and had someone read it to him. When the king heard the words of the book of the law, he tore his clothes and wept. He said, "Great is the wrath of the Lord that is kindled against us because of our Fathers. We have not obeyed the Words of this book to do according that all is written concerning us." Josiah gathered all the people and made a covenant before the Lord to keep the commandments and His testimonies with all his heart, all his soul, all his mind to perform the Words of this covenant written in this book.

He went throughout the land burning all the altars of the other gods—all the Ashtoreth poles, all the abominations of the other gods Moloch where children were sacrificed. He put away the mediums and the household gods, the idols, and all the abominations ever seen in the land of Judah and Jerusalem that he might establish the Words of the law written in the book that the priest found in the house of the Lord. "Put off your old self which belongs to your former way of life and is corrupt through deceitful desires. Put on the new self. Created within you after the likeness of God in true righteousness and holiness" (Ephesians 4:22, ESV).

So how do we access the presence of the Lord? First, we must purify ourselves. We must rid ourselves of all other gods, household gods, altars, and other gods of the TV and internet. Do we spend more time on Facebook than we do in the Word? Do we allow the god of Moloch to have the spirit of our children? To be sacrificed to the spirit of human trafficking? To the media of lustfulness, violence in the movies and games? Do we not guard our eye gates or ear gates? What do we allow into our home? What do we read? What do we hear? Whatever we allow into our eye gate or ear gate ends up in our heart. It becomes who we are. Yes, God allows us choices. But free-will, human-based choices do not keep us from the consequences of those choices.

The God of this world is real. He wages war against our very soul (mind, will, emotions). King Josiah heard the Word of the Lord and wept. Do we weep before God at the state of our country? At the state of our government? Do we act, or do we go along with it, to be politically correct? Or do we speak out and call sin what it is? Do we speak out against witchcraft in high places, mediums, racism and bigotry, rape? Or do we go along with the media and say, "It's this person's personal freedom to do those things"?

Webster's Dictionary defines *freedom*[1] as "The power to act or speak or think as one wants without hindrance or restraint." Have we been deceived by the God of this world, thinking our freedom gives us the right to trample other people's rights? Has the God of this world deceived us into think-

---

[1] "Freedom | Definition of Freedom," *Merriam-Webster*, accessed September 30, 2019, https://www.merriam-webster.com/dictionary/freedom.

ing freedom is racism, that we are free to rape, murder, sin, display bigotry, and divorce? "I want my freedom"—we hear the cry. Freedom without authority is not freedom. Godly freedom is personal integrity that starts where the other person's freedom stops. Personal integrity does not infringe on other boundaries. "Before Josiah there was no king like him. Who turned to the Lord with all his heart with all his soul and with all his might? According to the law of Moses nor did any like him arise after him" (2 Kings 23:25, NAS).

Can this be said about us—about our Christian walk, about our personal integrity, about our love of God? O Lord, let this be our prayer that others would see You through us, that we would obey Your Word and walk in personal integrity before You and others in our lives.

CHAPTER 9

Master Carpenter: A Parable on the Oil of the Spirit

The Carpenter steps down into his shop, pulling aside the curtains to let the light shine through to see what damaged pieces were brought into the shop for him, the Master Carpenter, to repair. As He looks around, He sees in a dark corner, where the light has failed to shine, a cabinet of original design that was made to hold beautiful things. However, over the years, life had buffeted its wood. Many scars and many splinters ran through the tired, dried wood. The Carpenter ran His fingers over the sacred wood. His finger happens upon a Creator stamp. A stamp burned into the wood. As He leans forward, tears come to His eyes. He realizes He was the Creator of this broken, splintered cabinet.

One day, the Master Carpenter Jesus, notices you on a back shelf. Darkness surrounds you from a lifetime of being buffeted by sin and shame. As He comes close, He wonders about each bruise, each wound, each shame. As He feels the tears again, He says, "You were not created for this" (Genesis

1:27, ESV). You were created in His own image. In the image and likeness of God you were created. As He works with gentle, loving hands, He speaks softly to your heart: "Let the spoken Word of Christ have his home within you dwelling in your heart and mind" (Colossians 3:16, AMP).

Christ, the Master Carpenter, reaches out and takes you from the shelf of pain. He wipes away your tears with the "oil of gladness." He fills the wounds with "the oil of the Rose of Sharon"—oil especially designed to heal wounds and cuts. Then He rubs it into your heart "frankincense and myrrh"—oil designed to heal the body and the mind. Finally, he rubs in the oil of "Balm of Gilead." This oil has an aspirin-like quality: anti-inflammatory. It is used to heal cuts and wounds in your spirit. "'It's not by might not by power but by my Spirit, (of which the oil is a symbol of the Holy Spirit) says the Lord of hosts,'" (Zechariah 4:6, ESV). "You have put on the new nature which is being renewed by the Holy Spirit after the image of your Creator" (Colossians 3:10, ESV).

CHAPTER 10

Spiritual Hoarding

In rebuilding my house, I had to clean out stuff, lots of stuff. Stuff from the past, stuff from the present, stuff I might need in the future. I never quite understood hoarding, but I began to see a spiritual analogy. We hoard *spiritually* and physically.

In our spiritual backpack, we keep stuff from the past. We hoard it; we cannot let go of it. It hurts—broken relationships, sexual abuse, emotional injuries, and sins of the past. Satan looks to keep us enslaved in our hoarding. There are questions like, "But what about…?" I could never forget what they did. We say, "The pain is too deep to let it go. You do not understand. They hurt me. They got the job I should have had." Emotional scars, we wear them like badges. We put Band-Aids on our hurts, alcohol, drugs, sexual sins. The list goes on, justifying our wounds. Hoarding becomes a need, a habit. We hoard our past stuff into the backpack which we carry into the present. We take all our broken wounds, our heavy rocks from our past, and stuff it down to add room for our present stuff (more wounds): relationships gone bad, hurts, wounds, present-day broken relationships, financial concerns, bitterness, and jealousy. In moving forward, we begin to hoard present-day rocks. We keep our defenses, of course. We might need them to help us hoard and protect our future stuff. Our spirits become heavy, oppressed, bent over by the weight of our hoarding. Sometimes we might even put a new roof on the house (i.e., a makeover, a new facelift), dye our hair, get our nails done. We change our outward appearances to protect our inward wounds, thinking people will not see what is on the inside.

Sometimes we will even drop our backpack in an emotional moment at the foot of the cross or in a church service. But when we leave, we pick it up and take it with us. There is no room for the fruit of the Spirit in our backpack. Jesus says, "Come to me all who labor and are heavy laden, I will give you rest. Take my yoke upon you, for my yoke is easy my burden light" (Matthew 11:28, ESV). Christ's joy is light and free. We need to let God cleanse our past, our spirits from stuff that weigh us down. It keeps us from having joy. We have so much stuff we are oppressed by it. We need to leave our burdens at the foot of the cross.

One day when we meet Christ at the foot of the cross, and the Holy Spirit moves in, the Spirit will clean house, saying, "What about tossing this? What about getting rid of that?" The Christian walk is a process, a journey. Little by little, the Holy Spirit points out things that we need to do to heal, to forgive, to say, "I am sorry," to take responsibility for our pain, for our part in the situation. It becomes not, "Lord, change them." It becomes, "Lord, change me. Help me let go of the past. Heal my wounds. Heal my relationships, past and present." "Therefore, confess your sins to one another and pray for one another, that you may be healed" (James 5:16, ESV).

What is taking place inside you is greater than what has come at you from the outside. A healing, a restoration, a cleansing, a renewing of your heart and soul and mind. "So now abide faith (abiding trust in God), hope (confident trust in his salvation), love (unselfish love for others), but the greatest of these is love" (1 Corinthians 13:13, AMP).

CHAPTER 11

Music Box

Life is spinning like a ballerina in a music box. Round and round, life spins. People spin each to his own sound, trying to make things right. Louder and louder the music grows as the evil one tries to get us to dance to his music, spinning out of control. I am dancing as fast as I can, but I cannot keep up. Then I hear it. I take just a moment to slow down. To breathe. I hear in the distance the sweet sound of another kind of music. His Spirit beckons me to hear. Somewhere deep within my soul, the music resounds. The music of heaven. We were made to worship. We were made to dance in joy to the music of heaven. Slow down, set your spirit free, and let your soul dance to the music of heaven.

CHAPTER 12

The Puppet Master

To the world, I am like a wooden puppet—happy, making others laugh—yet I am dry and dusty inside, being played by an evil puppet master for his evil schemes, using chains instead of rope. I have no choices; I feel no love inside, for my heart is hard. If my heart is dead to spiritual things, Satan, the puppet master, is happy. As he pulls the chains tighter, he laughs in the face of God.

But I cry out inside, *I want to be real. I want my hard wooden heart to be filled with the very breath of God, who, by His very hand, created me. Create in me a new heart.* "The Lord does not see as man sees; Man looks on the outward appearance, but the Lord looks on the heart" (1 Samuel 16:8, ESV). "You have put on the new nature. Which is being renewed by the Holy Spirit after the image of your Creator" (Colossians 3:10, ESV).

CHAPTER 13

Why Worship

Satan rejoices in the face of God at hardened hearts. He comes to steal, kill, and destroy. Worship puts a crack in the very heart of those whose heart Satan has hardened, oppressed, or filled with pride. "It is not the place which makes the true worship—it is the heart. It is not even the day—it is the state of a man's mind. Every place is equally holy—where holy men worship God" (Charles Spurgeon).[2] Christian worship becomes a seed planted between the rocks of a hardened spirit so that God's Spirit can grow in a person's heart. Satan was created a head musical angel. He understands full well the place of worship. That is where his point of pride began. "But you said in your heart I will ascend to heaven. I will raise my throne above the throne of God. I will make myself like the most high" (Isaiah 14:13, ESV).

We must worship the Creator, not the created, before we can understand God's Word. If we do not, we have had knowledge only. In church, worship comes before theology, opening the hearts of the people to the Spirit. Worship must

---

[2] "Short pithy gems from Spurgeon—Grace Gems!" accessed October 5, 2019, https://www.gracegems.org/30/short_pithy_gems_Spurgeon.htm.

come before theology so that our hearts are affected by the Spirit before our minds are informed so we may also receive heart knowledge. Worship becomes the bridge between head knowledge and the heart. We must teach people to worship in Spirit and truth. King David danced before the Lord with all his might in worship (2 Samuel 6:14, ESV), submitting to the Spirit of worship. "Jesus is my Lord and my God—and I will love and adore, and worship Him forever and ever!" (Charles Spurgeon)[3]

---

[3] Ibid.

CHAPTER 14

Eyeglasses

As I lay dreaming, I noticed a healing service in the chapel. As we started to pray, I saw an aged man leading up and down the aisles with a pillowcase, asking people to please put their eyeglasses in the pillowcase. At first, I did not understand the dream. Yet the dream did not go away; it remained in the back of my mind like still air. A few days later, I read Matthew 20:32 (ESV). The blind man said, "Son of David, have mercy on us." Jesus asked, "What do you want Me to do for you?" The blind man replied, "That our eyes be opened, Lord." My spirit jumped, and I thought, *Eyeglasses and eyes.* God created us with spiritual eyes and spiritual ears to see and hear things that are spiritually discerned. One of the phrases that Jesus used often was, "He who has ears, let them hear" (Matthew 11:15, NLT). He calls upon His people to open up their spiritual ears to hear what God is saying to them.[4] That is why it's so critical that we must safeguard what we see and hear.

---

[4] "Freedom from Fear: Seeing with Spiritual Eyes—Season of..." (September 5, 2010), accessed October 5, 2019. https://season.org/freedom-from-fear-seeing-with-spiritual-eyes/.

I started to pray, opening my eyes to see You, Lord. Awaken our spiritual eyes to see beyond the veil of the living. Oh, Lord, we cry out that we would see the grace of the Lord in the land of the breathing. Teach us to detect with our spiritual eyes and ears Your voice and Your vision. I felt God saying, *Wake up, My people, to the surrounding influences.* Let their eyes and ears be opened to the ways of the Spirit.

We must learn to shut out the evil influences around us in the media, the books we read, even the music that surrounds us. We are invaded by their prejudices. We must learn to replace them with worship music, and books that are pleasing to God. For above all else, what influences our eyes and ears influences our hearts. "Above all else guard your heart. For everything you do flows from it. The gateway to our heart is through our eyes and ears" (Proverbs 4:23, NIV).

CHAPTER 15

A Quiet Heart

As I sit beside the fireplace watching the flames of fire, I think of Your Holy fire rising in Your people. The fire of the Holy Spirit. You are mustering an army of anointed ones filled with the fire of Your Spirit. "The Lord of hosts is mustering His army for battle" (Isaiah 13:5, AMP). In the Old Testament, Your Spirit was a cloud by day and as fire by night. But now Your Spirit of the anointing lives within us; our strength comes from his Spirit within us. "We have an anointing from the Holy one" (1 John 2:20, NIV). Ephesians 6–11:16 (NIV) describes our spiritual armor. "Therefore, put on the full armor of God. So that you shall be able to resist and stand your ground in the day of evil." The armor only covers the front of us. Our complete covering comes from the Holy Spirit within us. We should be careful and aware of only going forward. We should never turn and run back to our old pathways, old habits, and old ways. We then become vulnerable to the enemy. We must move forward filled with the fire of the Holy Spirit within us. "In quietness with trust You will be our strength" (Isaiah 30:15, ESV). "The results of righteousness will be a peace, a quietness in my heart and confident trust forever in Your Spirit" (Isaiah 32:17, AMP).

CHAPTER 16

Intimacy with God is like marinating a
stew until it is tender to the Spirit.
—Author unknown

CHAPTER 17

Essential Elements

One of the most essential elements of a Christian is to have an intact secret relationship with the Father. "In the hidden place of my heart you make me know wisdom" (Psalms 51:6, ESV), those who spend time in his Word. "I would never have known the Savior's love half as much—if I had never been in the storms of affliction."[5]

Whether the storms originate from hell's fury or the world's distractions of finance, family, or illness, we waste far too much of our time on worldly matters! So many things can pull us away from finding time with the Father. "Be still and know that I am God; I will be exalted among the nation will be exalted in the earth" (Psalms 46:10, ESV). We exalt Him when we spend time with Him.

---

[5] "Short pithy gems from Spurgeon—Grace Gems!" accessed October 5, 2019, https://www.gracegems.org/30/short_pithy_gems_Spurgeon.htm.

CHAPTER 18

Light Exposes Darkness

Chaos and darkness surround me. I feel like I am living in the storm's eye. There is a light shining downward on me from You, though it would merely take a moment to step out of Your light into the swirling darkness. Walk with me, Father, on each step I take on this journey home. Light my path. Help me to remain close. The road home is filled with pitfalls and stones. Shine Your light around me one step at a time, lest my feet misstep in the chaos and darkness crashing in. "When you encounter the fog and your foot slips. You will only fall to the level of your relationship with the Father" (Christine Caine).[6] "When I thought my foot slipped your steadfast love upheld me. (Psalms 94:18, ESV). "Therefore, see that you walk carefully living life with purpose and courage not as the unwise but as a wise, sensible, intelligent, discerning person" (Ephesians 5:15, AMP).

---

[6] Christine Caine, "When the Unexpected Betrays," FaithGateway, accessed October 6, 2019, https://www.faithgateway.com/unexpected-betrays/.

CHAPTER 19

Storm Clouds

Father, draw us close. Cover us with Your wings. As a mother hen gathers her chicks from the coming storm as the lightning in the clouds gather, so shall Your Spirit gather Your people, Lord, to bring them to a safe place before the storm strikes. In Your Word, You say, "I will cover you and completely protect you. With my pinions under my wings you will find refuge" (Psalms 91:4, ESV).

Lord, as Your Spirit comes with thunder and strikes with your holy rod of justice, protect Your people as You can muster an army for battle. The darkness cannot stand the light. But with the anointing of Your Spirit, the light can withstand the darkness. Your Spirit Lord holds back the coming storm. As we hear and see rumblings in the distance, as the storm comes close, create in us an atmosphere to hear from You. Anoint our spiritual eyes and ears. For we, Your people, know Your voice. Create in us a surrendered heart and a bended knee. "'For I know the plans I have for you,' declares the Lord, 'plans for peace and well-being, not for disaster, but to give you a future and a hope'" (Jeremiah 29:11, AMP). Come quickly, Lord Jesus, come.

CHAPTER 20

Mended Hearts

Read this prayer titled "Hug the Little Girl Within Me"[7] by Melissa Taylor. I pray that this prayer speaks to your heart as it speaks to mine.

> Dear Father, hug the child within me. The child mistreated and abused. Encircle me today with Your loving arms. Still my silent unheard tears. Anoint my head with Your healing oil. Free me from nightmares of memories. Touch my scars with Your blood-stained healing stripes. Soothe each muscle that I suffered in anger and pain. Piece together my broken heart. In my sleepless nights wrap me in your comforting presence. Let me rest in the shadow of Your wings as You cover me with Your love like a mother hen covers her chicks.

---

[7] Melissa Taylor, "Hug the Little Girl within Me," accessed September 30, 2019, http://melissataylor.org/2010/08/19/hug-the-little-girl-within-me/.

He will cover you with his pinions under His wings you will find refuge (Psalms 91:4, NIV). Speak to my heart. Help me face yesterday (wrong as it was) and to forgive the wrongs done to my heart, both emotionally and physically. Help me look toward tomorrow with new love and hope.

"Mended Hearts" by Anita Corrine Donahue.[8]

---

[8] *Mended Heart: God's Healing for Your Broken Places*, Amazon, accessed October 7, 2019, https://www.amazon.com/Mended-Heart-Healing-Broken-Places/dp/080072495X.

CHAPTER 21

Oak Tree

A mighty oak tree starts out as the seed of an acorn, just as the Word of God is a seed planted in someone's heart. When we get saved, we do not become mighty oaks or spiritual giants overnight. New Christians need time to be discipled under spiritual authority. The problem is, we are in a culture of fast-track spirituality. We do not want to marinate in God's Word; we want instant growth such as a microwave. As the oak tree sprouts, it encounters much difficulty—being stepped on, being eaten, being ravaged by winter storms, scorched by the summer heat, being overtaken by disease. Each trial strengthens it. Without the trials, Christians would not grow into spiritual giants. "Do not surprised at the fiery trials when they come upon you to test your faith" (1 Peter 4:12, AMP). Just as an acorn needs to hide away in the earth for a period, new Christians must be hidden away under the protection and guidance of an elder, mature Christian.

Moses spent forty years in Egypt under Pharaoh, learning how to be a leader. He then spent forty years under his father in-law, Jethro, learning how to live in the very desert that he would later bring the Israelites through. David spent twenty years in the desert's backside learning to commune with God. David then spent twenty years under King Saul learning battle strategies before David himself became king.

The acceptance of Christ is only the beginning of the seed that has been planted in our hearts. To make us strong and grow, we must endure trials, storms, the freezing cold, and the scorching heat—the trials of life. "But even if you should suffer for righteousness' sake, you will be blessed" (1 Peter 3:14, ESV). Each lesson, each trial, each storm adds to our growth to strengthen us as Christians.

The taproot of the mighty oak tree must grow deep into the ground. As the tree grows outwardly, its roots must grow deep, searching for water and nutrients. As we grow spiritually, we must also sink our roots deep into the Word. We must search for the springs of living water. We must search the Word for nourishment to feed our spirits. Then we can grow and bear fruit. "Every healthy tree bears good fruit" (Matthew 7:17, ESV). Just as the mighty oak tree bears acorns that grow into beautiful oak trees, so should we bear the fruit of new Christians in our life.

Just as the mature oak tree shelters the new oak tree, we need to disciple and shepherd the new Christians. "Shepherd the flock of God that is among you exercising oversight" (1 Peter 5:2, ESV). "Then they shall become oaks of righteousness, (strong and magnificent, distinguished), planted by the Lord for the display of his Glory" (Isaiah 61:3, AMP).

CHAPTER 22

Pearl of Great Price

"You have kept count of my tossing you've put my tears in your bottle are they not in your book?" (Psalms 56:8, KJV). I believe God catches each of our tears in his bottle and holds them close to his heart. When this is done, He will, in His time, return them to us as a pearl of great price. Just as oysters need bits of sand to make a pearl, God uses our tears to make us a pearl of great price. After the trial, after the storm, and after the layers of life, that slowly forms the pearl. He releases something beautiful into our lives, so much so that our joy cannot contain it. "I will sing to the Lord a new song. For I rejoice in the Lord" (Psalms 104:33–34, AMP).

CHAPTER 23

The Perfect Storm

Darkness moves across the land, and storm clouds gather on the horizon. In this time of chaos, the waves of darkness threaten to overcome us as the perfect storm. We are drowning in a sea of political impurities. People are mixing the holy and the profane in their religion, in their relationships, and in their lives. As the darkness tries to pull us under, help us, Lord, to look up and see Your hand reaching down, grasping to pull us above the storm clouds. "Lord save me!" (Matthew 14:30, NIV). Immediately, Jesus reached out His hand and took hold of Matthew. "He made the storm be still. Let us thank him for his steadfast love" (Psalms 107:29, ESV). "I will not die Spiritually but live according to Your great mercy" (Psalms 118:17, AMP).

As we rise on eagles' wings, where the sun shines the brightest, we yield and submit ourselves to You, in agreement with You, to be conformed to Your will and be at peace. (The Hebrew definition of *peace* is "shalom")[9] "You are my God and I will give You thanks. You are my God and I will exalt

---

[9]   "The True Meaning of Shalom," accessed October 1, 2019, https://firm.org.il/learn/the-meaning-of-shalom/.

you" (Psalms 118:28, ESV). Help us to look up and reach for Your hand, Lord. Raise up the Davids in this Goliath world. Lord, who will come against this evil and will say, as David said to the giant Goliath, "I come against you in the name of the Lord of hosts, the God of Israel whom you have defied" (1 Samuel 17:23, AMP).

CHAPTER 24

Warfare

I pick up Your crown of thorns, which Your love for me cost You. War costs. We must count the cost carefully. War is a battle. A battle fought on a spiritual level between two unseen forces. It is a real battle between good and evil. It cost You, your life. What will cost me? What will I give up going to war to follow You into battle on bended knees? Family, friends, riches, and fame, the need to be known within religious circles.

You hung on the cross between two thieves. One thief said, "If You are the Son of God, throw Yourself down and us" (Matthew 4:6, NIV). He tempted Jesus and dared him to use His mighty power to escape. I seek Your hand to give me special attention. The second thief said, "You truly are the son of God. Remember me when you come into your kingdom." In other words, "I look up on Your bloodstained face and say, 'My Lord and my God, I will follow You even unto death.'" Peter was so humbled to be crucified like Jesus; he did not feel worthy. He asked to be crucified upside down. Ask yourself, What is this battle costing you? Which side of the cross do you find yourself on?

Father, as You muster an army to go into battle with You, make us known to the spirit world as Your servants ready to serve at a moment's notice with our sword and Your Word in our hand. Make us ready through Your Spirit to conquer the enemy spiritually with boots on the ground shod with the Gospel of peace.

If you had seen the shoes of a Roman soldier, you'd have wanted to make sure you didn't fall in front of him or get in his way where he might accidentally step on you. Those weren't normal shoes; they were killer shoes! They began at the top of the legs near the knees called "greaves" and extended down to the feet. They were made of metal and were specially shaped to wrap around the calves, safekeeping the soldier's legs. Just as those spikes held a Roman soldier securely in place when his enemy tried to push him around, the peace of God will hold you in place when the enemy tries to push you around! Paul continued, "And your feet shod with the preparation." The word *preparation* is the Greek word *etoimasin*, and it presents the idea of readiness or preparation. When used in connection with Roman soldiers, the word *etoimasin* portrayed men of war who had their shoes tied on very tightly to ensure a firm footing. Once they had the assurance that their shoes were going to stay in place, they were ready to march out onto the battlefield and confront the enemy.[10]

We hit the ground running with our sword and Your Word in our hands. Ready to conquer the enemy. In all circumstances of war, we take up the shield of faith to extinguish the darts of the enemy, our hearts and minds always praying in the spirit.

---

[10] "Are You Wearing Your Killer Shoes? | Rick Renner Ministries" (March 15, 2016), accessed October 6, 2019, https://renner.org/are-you-wearing-your-killer-shoes/.

CHAPTER 25

Awaken the Morning

Speak, Lord, for Your servant listens. As the sun rises over the horizon expectantly, I hear Your creation awakening at first light. I awaken as You stretch out the day before me. You are with me as I start my day. Throughout the day, Your Spirit talks to my spirit gently, binding me to do Your will. Fill me, Lord, with Your Spirit as my spirit awaits Your Word. You are the Lord, the Alpha and the Omega. There is no other. Besides You, there is no God. The rooster crows to awaken the dawn. "On your walls, O Jerusalem, I have set watchmen; all the day and all the night they shall never be silent. You who put the LORD in remembrance, take no rest" (Isaiah 62:6, ESV).

As I sit and contemplate the start of each new day, I go to Your Word and read about the watchmen on the wall. I hear You say to me, "Where are the watchmen on the wall? Why do they not cry out to awaken my people who slumber?" For in the atmosphere, the darkness is yet stirring as the morning dawns. As intercessors mount up as eagles and fly above the storm clouds, worshiping and praising Your name in a spirit of forgiveness and repentance.

The sun begins to shine rays of light into the darkness. "I have posted watchmen on your walls, O Jerusalem; They will never be silent day or night. You who call on the Lord, give yourselves no rest, and give him no rest till he established Jerusalem and makes her the praise of the earth" (Isaiah 62:6–7, ESV). In the light, Satan and his demons have no arsenal against forgiveness and repentance, which touches the very heart of God.

CHAPTER 26

The Shelter of the Most High God

"He who dwells in the shelter of the Most High will remain and rest in the shadow of the Almighty, whose power no enemy can withstand" (Psalms 91:14–15, ESV). Your Word says, "I will cover you and completely protect you with my pinions under my wings you will find refuge" (Psalms 91:14, ESV). Father, because You set Your love on me, I am confident You will save me. The Father says, "I will set you securely on high because you know my name you completely trust and rely on me knowing I would never abandon you" (Psalms 91:14, AMP). "You will call upon me and I will answer you" (Jeremiah 29:12, ESV).

As the waves of the evil one seeks to overcome me, I reach my hands up toward You in worship. You reach down and pull me up into Your presence. Oh, that I could stay in Your presence, Lord. But alas, the battle rages onward. My God, with great confidence I will rely on You. I will call upon You, and You will answer me. With a quiet heart, I will wait upon You. "Under your wings I will find refuge; your faithlessness is a shield and a wall about me" (Psalms 91:4, ESV). Fill me, Lord, with Your overflowing Spirit so it will spill over unto those around me—Spirit touching Spirit.

The day You died, blood and water flowed from the wound on Your side. The blood of redemption and the living waters flowed side by side as You hung on the cross Lord in place of me. God, You answered me with Your Word. "Because you hold fast to me, I will protect you. Because you know my name when I call on you. You will answer, I shall be with you in trouble I will rescue you and honor you" (Psalms 91:14, ESV).

CHAPTER 27

A Coal-Burning Locomotive

I sense something in the Spirit; a coal-burning locomotive engine appears in my mind. As prayer warriors, we are the coal shovelers, the people that shovel the coal secretly and unnoticed, maintaining the fire flame while the church runs full steam ahead—really, being virtually invisible to the church. And when "Jesus said, do not be like the hypocrites who walk and prayed to be seen by men; Truly they will be rewarded. What you do in secret is known by God and will be rewarded by God" (Matthew 6:5, BV).

And when we need to walk in our authority, we softly, carefully move in a way that Satan does not recognize how powerful we are. Like Navy Seals, we can be called to covert operations that cannot be shared except by a need-to-know basis.

CHAPTER 28

Consider the Redwood Trees

Consider the mighty redwood tree, the shortest of which is 350 feet tall. You would expect that the taproot of the redwood would extend deep into the ground. Yet the amazing redwood roots only grow five to eight feet deep. What supports the mighty redwood? The redwoods root spread out over one hundred feet in all directions, intertwining with the roots of the surrounding trees—intertwining to the extent you cannot dig through it. It is not the height that matters but the support of the other trees.[11] How in our Christian walk do we need to understand the metaphor here? The tangled roots support it from the ravages of nature like wind and storms. The root system makes it to stand tough against the storms of life. First Corinthians 12:27 (AMP) says, "Now you are Christ's body, and individually members of it." As Christians, how do we desire to be interwoven with one another? How do we need to support one another? Do you know your neighbors? Do you know the surrounding people

---

[11] "Redwood facts, or What Makes a Redwood Tree Grow?" accessed October 6, 2019, http://www.sunnyfortuna.com/explore/redwoods_and_water.htm.

who sit around you in church every Sunday? How would you support them in the ravages of their life? In our lives, we all seek for a support system. A support group, how awesome would it be that it be the church, the body of Christ?

The inside of the redwood tree is full of water, so much water that the bark of the tree is spongy. As the water ascends to the tips of the trees, it creates fog, which drips down into the branches and leaves and nourishes the root systems.[12] How, like us, as we ascend in worship, reaching up to touch heaven, the Holy Spirit moves over our lives and descends to touch lives around us, nourishing the roots of others.

"The heavens declare the glory of God. The sky above proclaims his handiwork. Day after day pours forth speech, and night after night shows forth knowledge" (Psalms 19:1–2, AMP). There is no speech in creation nor words whose voice is not heard. The very trees cry out, *There is a God.*

How humbling it would be to be part of the root system unseen, like intercessors in prayer, than to be the tree that is always seen but which cannot lead without the support of the intertwining root system.

---

[12] Ibid.

CHAPTER 29

Media Storm

The world swirls in chaos. The media surrounding us like a mighty storm, seeking to tell us how we should live. This generation seeks to change the Word of God to fit their desires, to set them free from rules and authority. "No rules for us," they cry. Do what you feel, let your passions carry you where you choose. Not for us, we are free from all the old ways. God, if You created us, why did You make me this way? So many questions. So many broken spirits. Darkness seeks to overshadow the light with chaos and confusion, yet the answers are found in the book of life. We just need to seek the one who, by the power of His Spirit, wrote it. "If anyone takes away from the Words of this book god will take away his share in the tree of life" (Revelations 22:19, ESV).

CHAPTER 30

Morning Praises

Lord, I could sit at Your feet forever. My heart is full. It cries out with praise, "Let everything that has breath praise the Lord" (Psalm 150:6, ESV). I listen for Your still, quiet voice today in a hundred ways. The songs of the morning birds, the rooster crowing to awaken the dawn, the morning sun rising with praises declaring Your glory at the dawn of a new day. I sense You in the morning wind as movement in the trees. "I tell you if these keep silent the very stones will cry out in praise" (Luke 19:40, ESV). "Worthy are You our Lord and our God. To receive glory, and honor and power. For you created all things" (Revelation 4:11, ESV). By Your will, they were created to praise You.

CHAPTER 31

Noah: A Story of Faith

There are many things we try to do without God. There are still things God will not do without us. God achieves His part by offering us wisdom and discernment. We must do our part with faith and obedience. "Let us draw near with a faithful heart in full assurance of faith" (Hebrews 10:22, ESV).

Are we calling for God to build an ark in our lives? Are we expecting miracles but not listening to His plan? He told Noah to build an ark and how to build it. But it was not God's plan to build the ark himself. God put lumber on trees. Noah walked by faith, but God directed him where to walk. "Your ears shall hear a word behind you saying this is the way walk in it. When you turn to the right or the left" (Isaiah 30:21, ESV). "By faith Noah, being warned by God concerning events as yet unseen, in reverent fear constructed an ark for the saving of his household" (Hebrews 11:7, ESV).

"When God patiently waited in the days of Noah while the ark was being prepared" (1 Peter 3:20, ESV). Like Noah, He waits for us to read and follow His written Word, which is the map to our journey home. While being guided by the moral compass of the Holy Spirit, like Christopher Columbus who discovered the new world by a physical compass, we need the spiritual navigation of the Holy Spirit to find our path home.

CHAPTER 32

Lighthouse

Definition of a lighthouse: "A lighthouse is a steady and grounded structure that guides people to safety. With a goal of guidance, it illuminates the darkest of times, bringing you love and hope. To guide them to safe harbor."[13] Years ago, someone lived in and managed the lighthouse. They used melted lard to keep the oil light going at all hours that the light might burn steadily.

What is the spiritual analogy here? Today we live in a raging world that is whirling around us in chaos. What is our guide or beacon of light? Do we have one? What tells us when we are getting off course in our lives, when it seems we are about to be shipwrecked and lose everything we have, maybe even our very lives? God looked down and saw the world was in chaos and getting off course. He sent His prophets to give us the law. But it was not enough. People's hearts remained in darkness, hard and unchanging. He sent His Son as the light. He sent His Spirit to guide and direct us through His Word.

---

[13] "The Sacred Symbolism of the Lighthouse—The Alex and...," accessed October 1, 2019, https://blog.alexandani.com/symbolism-and-meaning-of-lighthouses/.

"I am the light of the world that shines in the darkness" (John 9:5, NIV). "The people living in darkness have seen a great light" (Matthew 4:16, NIV). "The people who walked in darkness have seen a great light; those who dwelt in a land of deep darkness on them a light has shown" (Isaiah 9:2, ESV). After Jesus's ascent, God sent His Holy Spirit to live in us to be a light. "You are the light of the world let Your light shine" (Matthew 5:14). "We have the fire, the Holy Spirit in us. Tongues of fire appeared to them and rested on each of them" (Acts 2:3, ESV). His Spirit dwells within us, keeping us as the lightkeeper to keep the oil of the Spirit burning.

His Spirit dwells within us to guide and direct others as a beacon of light—to guide others to Him, a safe harbor during the roaring storms of life. Life has many storms swirling around us. Each is unique to that person, be it personal or political. The storms of life are real once it is total chaos, and we feel we cannot endure the storm. *I have not called you out of the darkness to curse the darkness. I have called you to be a light into the darkness so that there is a way that people can see beyond the absolute darkness of their lives. So let your light shine as a beacon to a stormy world—or be as lights on a runway bringing My people home.*

My prayer is "that I may walk before the Lord in the light of life" (Psalms 56:13, ESV). My prayer for you is, "Lord lift up the light of your face upon us" (Psalms 4:6, AMP).

CHAPTER 33

We Are Called

"I set watchmen on the wall over you speaking. Listen and pay attention to the warning sound of the trumpet (shofar)" (Jeremiah 6:17, NIV). As the dawn breaks the morning sky, as the rooster stirs to awaken the day, God calls forth His watchmen to awaken His people from their slumbering. The watchmen around the city of Jerusalem had three watches: sunset to 10:00 p.m., 10:00 p.m. to 2:00 a.m., 2:00 a.m. to sunrise. We must choose our watch in the Spirit. Dutch Sheets calls us to the spiritual wall to stand guard over the safeguard of our homes, our cities, our nations.

Tommy Tenny speaks on this subject: "Our Spiritual survival often hangs by a slender thread. Dependent on the Spiritual eyesight of the watchmen on the wall. A watchmen's prayer is like a vitamin to their Spiritual eyesight."[14]

An intercessor's prayer is not just a few trite words spoken over someone; it is a lifestyle, devoted to our families, our cities, and our nations. Led by the Holy Spirit, a watch-

---

[14] "From Dutch Sheets, 'Watchman Prayer,'" accessed October 1, 2019. https://irp-cdn.multiscreensite.com/c21a6153/files/uploaded/ Watchman%20Prayer%20-%20by%20Dutch%20Sheets.pdf.

man's prayers play an important role in drawing a perimeter of protection around our families, including our church families, our cities, and our nation. "Listen you who wonder, for I will do something in your day that you would never believe even if someone had told you" (Acts 13:41, NIV).

A single prayer like one drop of rain cannot quench the thirst of the people spiritually, but many prayers combined, like much rain, can flood a city with the glory of God. We today are being called to be watchmen on the wall. It is seen as a spiritual metaphor, but it is truly real. It is our spiritual obedience that gives us the honor to be called "watchmen on the wall." We must, as watchmen on the wall, take our place to call out, to prepare us of the dangers ahead, spiritually and physically.

CHAPTER 34

The Cross

The darkness is filled with shadows as I awake before dawn. Even the rooster is still sleeping. I worship You in the morning's darkness at the foot of the cross. You lead me out of the shadows as the darkness vanishes before the morning light. The cross where darkness and light clashed so many generations ago vying for the sons of earth, where You battled for the sons of earth with Your very life, opened my spiritual eyes to see and understand. Your very angels standing by, weeping. "Do you not think I could appeal to my Father, and he will at once send me twelve legions of angels" (Matthew 26:52, ESV). There were twelve legions of angels awaiting the spoken Word that they could avenge His Son, their Lord. You could have called down the very forces of light. Instead, You whispered with Your very last breath, "Father, forgive them for they know not what they do" (Luke 23:34, ESV).

CHAPTER 35

A Single Candle

Father, lift us up with our spiritual eyes to see above the darkness, to see things as You see them. Grant our hearts a love for the people in darkness. Satan has captured them with invisible chains with lies and deceit. You reached down into the darkness of this world with a single candle of light by sending Your Son. One person filled with a fire of the Holy Spirit can bring light into the darkness. Just as one match can start a firestorm, use us to bring light into the darkness. Lord, teach us how to light new candles with the flame of Your Holy Spirit as on the day of Pentecost that they too can have Your light, Your Holy Spirit, and illuminate the very atmosphere around them.

Father, shine Your light in the dry, dusty religious places of our heart. Awaken our Spirits to hear, to listen to Your Spirit whisper, "Come forth into the light awaken your slumbering Spirit" (Isaiah 49:6, ESV).

A darkness walks across the land. It marches forth, throwing chaos into our paths. Awaken Your Spirit within us by the anointing of the Holy Spirit to battle with the king of darkness. Your Word says in Judges, "I have called you out of darkness not to curse the darkness but to bring light into the darkness that blinds my people." Teach us to say as David did before Goliath, "I come in the name of the Lord of hosts" (1 Samuel 17:45, ESV). Teach us to stand before the enemy with the light of your love. Against such there is no law. Against such love the darkness cannot stand.

"For once you were in darkness, but now you are a light for the Lord; walk as children of the light" (Ephesians 5:8, ESV). "All things become visible when they are exposed by the light for God is light. In him there is no darkness" (Ephesians 5:13, ESV). Spiritually speaking, as a believer functions in the light, He will expose the sins of unbelievers simply by His presence—just as it is in the nature of light to expose whatever it touches.

CHAPTER 36

Speak, Lord, for Your Servant Listens

As I awaken in the predawn, I hear you whisper, *Come sit with me awhile.* Together we can command the day. Together Your Spirit in me whispers, *Rise up. The watch begins.* Even before the rooster crows, my Spirit awakens. You whisper, *Come sit with me awhile. Open up your Spirit to Me in the quiet, in the silence.* As I listen, You speak to my Spirit, *It's not the distance that separates us. It's the silence of your soul where you've shut Me out. You give Me yourself in prayer, you give Me your heart, yet the silence hidden away in your soul creates a distance between us. Deep within your soul, the wound stays. The wounds have been stuffed down. Your voice cries out in prayer to Me, "Help me." Yet you are afraid to let go. Your soul is where the many wounds are. Your soul is where I desire to come—the hurts, the pain, even the struggles you have forgotten residing there.*

Again I hear you whisper, *Come sit with me awhile. I long to comfort you, to call you My friend, to share the deep things. Open the door, my friend. Let me in, I stand at the door to your soul, knocking. I will not forsake you.*

"Do not forget my teachings. Let your heart keep my commandments for length of days and years of life and peace they will add to your life" (Psalms 3:1, ESV).

Come sit with me awhile.

"He will cover with his feathers" (Psalms 91:4, NIV). He will sooth with his Words. "His faithful promises are your Spiritual armor and protection" (Psalms 91:4, NIV). Your Spirit whispers, "Come, sit with me awhile."

CHAPTER 37

Our Children

I see parents, pastors, teachers on their knees crying out for our youth. Even the very young are being attacked before birth. Hitler said, "I want to raise a generation of young people devoid of conscience, imperious, relentless, and cruel."[15] Soldiers on their knees crying out, "Father, do You see? Do You hear?" As we wrestle in the night with the powers of darkness, raise up warriors, Lord, who, like David, will run to meet the enemy with the name of the Lord of hosts on their side. Call out Your people. Call them to do battle on their knees as the battle rages on.

So many questions, Father. We cry out as parents, "When will it end?" With broken hearts, we weep before Your throne. We cry out for our children, "Save them, Lord. Show us how to do battle, Lord, in this war against our children. Show us how to use our sword, the Word, to call forth the mighty angels to guard Your heritage." Your Word says in Malachi 2:15 (ESV), "What is the one thing God is seeking? Godly offspring."

---

[15] "Talk: Adolf Hitler," Wikiquote, accessed October 1, 2019, https://en.wikiquote.org/wiki/Talk:Adolf_Hitler.

Raise up watchmen on the wall to give a warning call. Let them sound their trumpets calling people to pray. As the battle rages around us, we cry out, "Release our children from the darkness." Release them from the very tentacles of Satan that seek to pull them under into the depths of darkness. We cry out, "Lord, do You hear me? Do You see me?"

CHAPTER 38

Good morning, Father. The morning watchmen take their stand on the wall, awaking Your people. Father, call them out of slumber. With sleep still in their eyes, they rise to take their place on the wall. They ascend first into Your throne room to worship to be filled with Your Spirit. Awaken them with power and strength as they descend to battle, guarding Your people, Your cities, and Your nation. For the kingdom of God is not a matter of talk but of wisdom and power. "The God of Jacob Is our stronghold. Our refuge, our high tower" (Psalms 46:10, ESV). "God will help his people when the morning dawns" (Psalms 46:5, ESV). A new day begins.

CHAPTER 39

As Joshua

In Joshua 1:5 (NIV), God spoke to him, "Joshua just as I was with Moses so I will be with you. I will not leave you nor forsake you. The Lord your God is with you wherever you go. Only be strong and courageous for you will cause the people to inherit the land that I swore to your forefathers" (Joshua 1:9, NIV). "Be careful to do everything according to the law of Moses commanded you" (Joshua 1:8, ESV). We must be in the Word; we must spend time with God to know His promises. You must ponder on it day and night. God said to Joshua, "See now the Lord your God is with you wherever you go. You need not fight the battles you are fighting against this great swarm of demons. You need not be afraid for the Lord your God is with you wherever go." "The definition of strong in Hebrew is; to be or grow firm or strong, strengthen. The transliteration: chazaq, phonetic spelling: (khaw-zak')."[16] "The definition of Courageous in Hebrew is;

---

[16] "Strong's Hebrew: 2388. חָזַק (chazaq)—to be or grow firm or...," accessed October 1, 2019, https://biblehub.com/hebrew/2388.htm.

to be stout, strong, bold, alert. The transliteration: amets, phonetic spelling: (aw-mats').''[17]

What demons are you fighting? Depression, anger, lust, drugs, smut, financial troubles, physical ailments, family issues? Be strong. Secure yourself firmly. Read the Word daily. "Be not afraid. Be not dismayed by this great horde for the battle is not yours but the Lord's" (2 Chronicles 20:15, ESV). "You will not need to fight this battle. Stand firm" (2 Chronicles 20:17, ESV). Remember, *strong* in Hebrew means "to determine, to stand firm." *Courage* means "to firmly hold your position and see the salvation of the Lord on your behalf."

---

[17] "Strong's Hebrew: 553. אָמֵץ (amets)—to be stout, strong, bold…," accessed October 1, 2019, https://biblehub.com/hebrew/553.htm.

CHAPTER 40

As the Rooster Crows

I praise You this morning, Lord, as the rooster begins to call the sun to rise. I asked for Your blessings on this day. Your Word says, "Incline your ear to the words of my mouth and be willing to learn. That you may teach about the need to nurture the next generation" (Psalms 78:1, ESV). Your Word says we should nurture from the older to the younger. The younger generation needs nourishing in the ways of the Spirit. "Incline your ear to the words of my mouth. I will utter sayings from of old. We will not hide them from our children that which we have known and heard. But we will tell the next generation the praiseworthy deeds of the Lord" (Psalms 78:2–4, NIV). They need to learn to accept spiritual authority, not just approval of what their plans are. They need to develop a mantle of wisdom and graciousness, to learn how to submit to the authority and die to themselves. If they are not taught, how will they learn? How will they learn if it is not modeled in front of them? Do we live our lives in such a way that, without words, our lives say, "Come and see, I have found Him, the Son of God"? We as mature Christians should tell the next generation of God's great, mighty power and the wonderful works He has done so that the generation yet to be born may arise and recount them to their children that they too may place their confidence in God.

CHAPTER 41

Finding God

Where can I find You, Lord? I go into the deep; You are not there. I enter into the heavens; I could not find You. Then in my heart, I sense Your presence. I find Your Spirit residing inside me. "For He dwells within you and will be in you" (John 14:17, NIV). "He breathed upon them and said receive the Holy Spirit. May peace (a quiet heart) be within you. As the Father has sent me so I send you" (John 20:21, NIV). Remind me daily that Your Spirit resides within me.

Teach me to walk according to Your Word. In a spirit of holiness, anoint Your Words, Lord, that others may understand, that they also may experience Your presence. Let my heart become one with Your heart, two hearts beating as one. As a wife submits to her husband, so shall I submit to You. "Obey those who rule over you, and be submissive, for they watch out for your souls, as those who must give account. Let them do so with joy and not with grief, for that would be unprofitable for you" (Hebrews 13:17, NKJV). He is our covering, and in order to stay under covering, we must be walking with Him in obedience. "If the Lord has placed a leader 'over' us, then we must submit ourselves to the Lord's process."[18] I listen for Your voice in the early dawn, before the day awakens. Create in me clean hands and a pure heart so that through Your Spirit, Lord, I may enter Your presence.

---

[18] "Spiritual Covering and Authority," Burning Point Ministries, accessed October 1, 2019, http://www.burningpointministries.com/spiritual-covering-and-authority.

CHAPTER 42

King's Highway

I see flaming torches being lit each from God's Spirit one at a time along the King's highway. Carrying each torch, lit by the flame of the Spirit, is a prayer warrior lighting the way home. As they advance, calling each to his place on the wall, the flames grow brighter. The way home is traveled by His faithful, bringing His people home.

CHAPTER 43

Spiritual Eyes

Open my spiritual eyes that I may see beyond the veil that separates us. My Spirit longs to ascend to Your throne room that I may sing with the angels, "Holy, holy, holy is the Lord almighty." "Your word is a lamp for my feet, a light on my path" (Psalms 119:105, NIV). Who has clean hands and a pure heart? Who keeps the Sabbath and does not profane it? These, will I bring to my holy mountain. They will make a joyful noise in my house of prayer. "Incline your ear and come to me That your soul may live" (Isaiah 55:3, NIV). "Wake yourself! Wake yourself up!" (Isaiah 51:17, NIV). Put on God's strength. Shout for joy, for the Lord is our strength.

CHAPTER 44

"Who shall ascend the hill of the Lord? Who shall stand in his Holy place? He who has clean hands and a pure heart" (Psalms 24:3–5, ESV). One who does not lift up his soul to what is false and does not swear deceitfully. One who is "pure in heart" or "purehearted" is without malice, treachery, without evil intent, honest with no hypocrisy.[19] Given our human condition, how do we attain this standard? The very thing we struggle for is that we may live our life in such a way to see God. A pure heart is not divided or double-minded. Everything in our lives should rotate around the glory of God. This is much like our lives which rotate around the sun. We may not pay attention to it, but the sun greatly influences our lives. This journey or pathway is called purity of heart. "Blessed are the pure in heart for they will see God" (Matthew 5:8, ESV). "They will see his face" (Revelations 22:4, ESV).

We on our own cannot obtain purity. Our journey is not perfection but a journey with a heart that seeks God day

---

[19] "Purehearted | Definition," Dictionary.com., accessed October 6, 2019, https://www.dictionary.com/browse/purehearted.

by day, of letting God smelt us like the silversmith, skimming off what is polluted (our sins) called dross, until the Maker sees his face in us. All the influences in our lives that do not please God one by one will be smelted out. Purity of heart is not something we obtain instantly. It is a day-by-day effort, each situation and each circumstance being given over to God. We need to respond to God daily with purity of heart, which is a daily examination of our heart at the soul level.

Purity of heart speaks about the ways we give God our heart inwardly. Where is the loyalty of our hearts? Many people do not understand that only with God's grace can we become pure in heart. God operates at the heart level. He sees the fissures, the cracks, the divisions that produce character flaws. Positive thinking is us trying to obtain purity of heart without the Holy Spirit or grace of God. It is fruitless. It is a day-by-day surrender of our rights to the Spirit of God. This is the journey we must undergo to ascend to the mount of God.

We need to seek God until all the world has to offer is pale in the light of God's glory. "Blessed (anticipating God's presence, spiritually mature) are the pure in heart (those with integrity, moral courage, and godly character), for they will see God" (Matthew 5:8, AMP). Without seeking to be pure, we will begin to despise instead of treasure God's teaching on this critical, crucial topic.

Many people, including pastors or teachers, become content with an outward show of a pure heart. But God through Jesus looks upon the heart of man. "Do not look on his appearance or the height of his stature. Because I have rejected him for the Lord sees not as a man sees. Man looks on the outward appearance, but the Lord looks on the heart" (1 Samuel 16:71, ESV) "Beloved if our hearts do not condemn us (of guilt) we have confidence (complete assurance and boldness) before God" (1 John 3:21, AMP). The loyalty of our heart betrays the weakness of one's life. Satan knows the weaknesses of our heart. He knows which buttons to push to cause us not to have loyalty of heart to God but to have a divided heart. Being pure does not mean being without flaws. "Create in me a clean heart oh God. Renew a right and steadfast Spirit within me. Restore unto me the joy of your salvation" (Psalms 51:10–12, ESV). "Blessed are the pure in heart for they shall see God" (Matthew 5:8, ESV).

CHAPTER 45

As the Eagle Rises

As the eagle rises to meet the morning sun, may my prayers rise as incense before You. My spirit rises to touch the dawn. In peace with the eyes of an eagle, I ride the wind of Your spirit. With Your peace inside me, I feel I can touch the very edge of heaven. Oh, that I may touch the hem of Your garment to bring healing to this world. For only through Your peace, Your healing, can your people survive the storm. Come, Holy Spirit, fill this day with Your glory. "I extol and praise you. For you oh Lord have lifted me up" (Psalms 30:1, NIV). My soul shall sing Your praises and not be silent. Oh, Lord, my God, I will give thanks to You forever.

CHAPTER 46

Curtting

I find that at the first hint of emotion, I retreat like a turtle into my shell in panic. After all, if I do not feel it, I do not have to deal with it, right? Emotions are a hard thing to control. Do we weep silently in our soul, or do we shout out to others in panic? "Put the cap back on. Your emotions are spilling out." Do people see us as wildly emotional or shut in ourselves and very stoic? How does God sees us? "God sees not as man sees. Man looks on the outward appearance. But the Lord looks on the heart" (1 Samuel 16:7, ESV).

How is your heart today? Hardened with guile and anger, caught up in the emotions of the day? Or do you have a quiet heart before God and people. Do you have peace? "Be still and know that I am God" (Psalms 46:10, NIV). The Hebrew word for "peace" is *shalom*, which is derived from a root denoting wholeness or completeness, and its frame of reference throughout Jewish literature is bound up with the notion of *shelemut*, "perfection."[20]

---

[20] "Shalom: Peace in Hebrew," My Jewish Learning," accessed October 6, 2019, https://www.myjewishlearning.com/article/shalom/.

CHAPTER 47

Cindi Jacobs notes in *Worship Warrior* by Chuck Pierce that the first thing we have to do is not to check our weapons but check our hearts to make sure the sinful nature's been cut away by Christ.[21] This releases us into the next phase of war and intercession. God told the Israelites they could not stand up before their enemies without consecrated hearts (Joshua 7:13, NIV). Consecrate yourself, for thus—the Lord God of Israel says—you cannot stand before your enemies until you have removed the things from under the ban. "Consecration is the Hebrew Word (KAW-dash) which means to be morally clean this suggests we are to be separated from the world around us Satan wants to take true worship out of the church the war is over worship our Spirit does one of two things it

---

21   *The Worship Warrior: Ascending in Worship, Descending in War*, accessed October 7, 2019, https://books.google.com/books/about/The_Worship_Warrior.html?id=TY99bK2cmDUC.

dies within us or comes to life. legalism our flesh is ministered to but our Spirits wither and die within us."[22]

God's Spirit falls and begins to prosper. Take your tambourines, take them down, and begin to worship. With tambourines and harps, I will praise. He broke the power of death. With tambourines and harps, I will raise the song of victory. Tambourines and praise, I will sing until the King is broken forth with strength, victory. It is through the praises of his saints that God springs into action. "God has ascended among the sounding of the trumpets (shofar). God arises God launches forth from our worship every blow of the rod of punishment the Lord lays on Satan launches forth from our praise" (Psalms 47:1–5, NIV). "Clap your hands all you nations shout to God with cries of joy" (Psalms 47:1–5, NIV).

How awesome is the Lord Most High, the Great King over all the earth. He subdues nations under our feet. He chose our inheritance for us, the pride of Jacob whom he loved. God has ascended among shouts of joy. The Lord has ascended among the sounding of the trumpets (shofar), singing praises to God. Sing praise to God, sing praise to our King. Sing praises, for the kings of the earth belong to God. He is greatly exalted. Every stroke the Lord lays on the enemy will be to the music of tambourines and harps as he fights him in battle with the blows of his mighty arm.

[22] "H6942—qadash," Strong's Hebrew Lexicon (KJV)," accessed October 1, 2019, https://www.blueletterbible.org/lang/lexicon/lexicon.cfm?t=kjv&strongs=h6942.

CHAPTER 48

Be Strong and Courageous

In the book of Joshua, God says to him, "Just as I was with Moses so I shall be with you. I will not leave you nor forsake you" (Joshua 1:5, ESV). "Be strong and courageous, for you shall cause my people to inherit the land that I swore to your forefathers" (Joshua 1:6, NIV). "Only be strong and courageous being careful to do all according to the law" (Joshua 1:7, NIV).

Throughout the book of Joshua, God continued to encourage Joshua spiritually and physically before entering a war with pagan warriors and demon giants.[23] Sometimes we need to ask God to refill us with His strength, to prepare us for the challenges ahead. "Do not be afraid and do not be dismayed, for I am your God" (Isaiah 41:10, ESV). Be strong, stand firm on the promises of God. God says in Joshua, "See now that I am He; there is no God beside Me" (Deuteronomy 32:29, BSB).

---

[23] "God's Promise to Joshua and Believers: A Bible…Patheos" (19 Apr. 2017), accessed October 1, 2019. https://www.patheos.com/blogs/christiancrier/2017/04/19/gods-promise-to-joshua-and-believers-a-bible-study-and-commentary/.

You do not need to fight the battles you are fighting—depression, anger, lust, to name a few. What battles of this great horde of demons are you facing? "When Joshua was in Jericho, he suddenly saw a man standing in front of him, holding a sword. Joshua went up to him and He asked, "Are you on our side or on the enemies' side?" (Joshua 5:13, CEV). "The man answered, 'Neither, but as commander of the army of the Lord'" (Joshua 5:14, NIV). Make up your own mind to be strong and courageous, to stand firm, allowing God to fill you with His strength. Be strong and stand firm on the promises of God.

CHAPTER 49

As the Rooster Crows

I praise you this morning, Lord, as the rooster begins to call the sun to rise. I asked for Your blessings on this day. Your Word says, "Incline your ear to the Words of my mouth and be willing to learn. That you may teach about the need to nurture the next generation" (Psalms 78:1, AMP). Your Word says we should nurture by the older to the younger. "We will tell to the next generation the praiseworthy deeds of the Lord" (Psalms 78:4, AMP). The younger generation needs nourishing in the things of the Spirit. "That our fathers have told us. I will utter sayings from of old" (Psalms 78:2–4, AMP). We will not hide them from our children that which we have known and heard. They need to learn to accept spiritual authority, not just approval of what their plans are. They need to develop a mantle of wisdom and graciousness, to learn how to submit to the authority over them. If they are not taught, how will they learn? How will they learn if it is not modeled in front of them? Do we live our lives in such a way that, without words, our lives say, "Come and see, I have found Him, the Son of God"? We as mature Christians should tell the next generation of God's great might and power and the wonderful work he has done that the generation yet to be born may arise and recount them to their children—that they too may place their confidence in God.

CHAPTER 50

Bitter in Spirit

At the waters of Meribah, the Lord spoke to Moses, saying, "Take your staff, and assemble the congregation, you and Aaron your brother, tell the rock before their eyes to yield its water." Moses took the staff from before the Lord as He commanded him. Moses and Aaron gathered the assembly together before the rock, and he said to them, "Hear now, you rebel: shall we bring water for you out of this rock?" And Moses lifted his hand in anger and struck the rock with his staff twice instead of speaking to it, and water came out abundantly. The Lord said to Moses and Aaron, "Because you did not believe in me, to uphold me as Holy in the eyes of the people of Israel, therefore you shall not bring this assembly into the promised land that I've given them" (Numbers 20:5–15, NIV).

Moses, even with me the Lord was angry on your account and said, "You shall not go into the promised land" (Deuteronomy 32:51–52, NIV). Joshua stands before you. Encourage him, for he shall lead Israel to inherit it. Moses became what the Word tells us. He became bitter in spirit because of the people. Moses got so bitter he disobeyed God.

It overtook him to the point of disobedience. He didn't get to lead the people into the Promised Land. Was it because he disobeyed God and struck the rock? Or because God saw the root of a deeper problem? Moses let bitterness invade his soul, his spirit. Could that be why God was angry? If he had obeyed, the people would have seen a loving side of a holy, miraculous God. Instead, they saw an angry, fleshly man. The miracles happened, but the reward was not the same. It did not reap an awe, a respect, for a Holy God.

Bitterness of the soul can carry us through life, like Ishmael, the firstborn of Abraham. In Genesis 16, Haggai developed a bitter spirit. Through tragic circumstances, Ishmael lost his birthright as the eldest son, and he remained bitter all his life because of not receiving what he thought was rightfully his. Isaac became the heir of the covenant promise. Down through generations, the spirit of bitterness dwells. We see it today as they cry, "Abraham is our Father." Bitterness, hate, jealousy corrupt the soul. The fight rages today. We see it in the Mideast between Israel the Jews and all the descendants of Ishmael. The power struggle, the family hate rages. But the battle is deeper and unseen. It's a battle over the soul. In the story of Abraham, God had a plan, a covenant, and a promise. A chosen bloodline. Satan tried to circumvent that plan.

Personal history. Do we let bitterness overcome us, doing damage to our spirit, not letting the spirit of God show others how Holy he is? Maybe people or families that we know are Christians. Yet we get so angry with people that it eats at our very soul and tears apart our families, tears apart governments and cities and nations. Anger and bitterness are, after all, a choice we make. When it comes deep down, it is really a mature choice. Family drives us crazy with bitterness, anger, jealousy; we get tired of the fighting. Moses got tired of the squabbling, the fighting. He struck back; he reacted out of anger. He lost the reward of going into the Promised Land. Although very angry with the Jews, Moses still was held accountable for his behavior. Then Moses and Aaron gathered the community together in front of the rock. "Pay attention, you rebels!" Moses told them. "Are we to bring you water from this rock?" (Numbers 20:12, ESV). What do we lose when we react, when we become bitter, when we let ourselves become overwhelmed? What are the consequences to our spiritual life? We lose sight of the promise of peace and joy. The real promise is peace and joy in Jesus Christ. We can have peace and joy knowing the promises of God, or we can have bitterness and discord, which will destroy our very soul.

CHAPTER 51

Birds of a Feather

Birds have feet and can walk. Birds have talons to grasp the branches securely. That was designed before their birth, but not until they fly are they living at their optimum, what they were God-given designed for (Chuck Pierce).[24] Just as birds were built to fly, we were created to worship. Naturally, we worship things, places, people, and fame. In our desire to worship, we worship dead idols such as the golden calf in Exodus. We worship many idols in our life, things that are more important to us than our living God.

> Until we worship as an act of the will and our Spirits begin to awaken inside us. Until our soul begins to live with our God-given desire to worship. A new flow of anointing will not flow. We can read Spiritual books, we can walk in ministry, we can even teach. We can run with

---

[24] *The Worship Warrior: Ascending in Worship, Descending in War*, accessed October 7, 2019, https://books.google.com/books/about/The_ Worship_Warrior.html?id=TY99bK2cmDUC.

busyness. But until we worship, we are not living at our God-given anointed best. (Chuck Pierce)[25]

Ascribe to the Lord, O heavenly beings, ascribe to the Lord glory and strength. Ascribe to the Lord the glory due his name; worship the Lord in the splendor of holiness. (Psalms 29:1–2, ESV)

Oh come, let us worship and bow down; let us kneel before the Lord, our Maker! For he is our God, and we are the people of his pasture, and the sheep of his hand. Today, if you hear his voice. (Psalms 95:6–7, ESV)

I appeal to you therefore, brothers, by the mercies of God, to present your bodies as a living sacrifice, holy and acceptable to God, which is your spiritual worship. (Romans 12:1, ESV)

---

[25] Ibid.

CHAPTER 52

Unity in Spirit

A flock of geese winging its way across the sky in unison can serve to remind us that when a person comes under the authority of the leader at the helm who has sacrificed his/her individual ego to the larger vision of the group. When the leader is truly called to the God-given position of leadership, we must come under his/her authority. A leader who sees the larger vision instills in his/her followers a sense of the Holy Spirit moving in a new and refreshing way. We must also as followers surrender our egos and pride to the unison of becoming united in one purpose. We must come with a surrendered heart and bended knee to the Holy Spirit that directs and guides the group so that we may like the flock of geese move in unison. "Therefore, bear with one another in love eager to maintain the unity of the Spirit in the bond of peace" (Ephesians 4:2, ESV).

CHAPTER 53

Two Kings

This earth is not our home. We are on a journey toward home. As we travel to a far country, two kings battle for our soul. The king of darkness and the King of light. Darkness beckons us with a sense of worldly independence, a sense of pleasures unlimited. We turn our backs on the King of light. After all, what does He, the King of light, have to offer? We say, "What about me?" Obedience, rules? "Because you are lukewarm, I will spit you out of my mouth. You say I am rich. I have prospered and have need of nothing. Yet You do not know that you are wretched and blind without hope" (Revelations 3:17, ESV). Satan whispers in your ear, "See, no one loves you."

As you turn toward the darkness, the king of darkness inserts daily a skeleton key deeper and deeper, shutting out the light into our hearts. Claiming victory, the king of darkness laughs in the face of the King of light. "How can you redeem her? Buy her back? You are a God of holiness. She is covered with sin and shame. You cannot even look upon her. One more twist of the key, and she is mine. Her spirit begins to die within her." Spiritual death—the ultimate betrayal to the King of light. A broken heart worn down by the ravages of time, broken and bruised. You shed a tear. Your childlike heart is broken. "The Lord is close to the broken hearted he saves those who are crushed in Spirit" (Psalms 34:18, ESV). Do You see our tears we shed in darkness sometimes in silence, You who created us? Yes! The King of light longs to wipe away each tear. Knowing that the King of light longs to redeem us, to buy us back from slavery to the king of darkness, Satan demands a sacrifice, the ultimate sacrifice of blood. *The King's son*—the king of darkness will settle for nothing less.

The King of light says to the king of darkness, "Take note, I will make Myself known to those of the king of darkness. I will say to those who come into the light through the death of My Son, who is the final sacrifice, 'Come and bow down at My feet. I will make known to you without any doubt that I love you, that I have set you free from darkness. I have given to those who are obedient and keep My Word the keys to the kingdom of light."

"I will make all his way straight. My Son, will rebuild my city and set the exiles free" (Isaiah 45:13). "There will be no need of lamp or sun, for the Lord God will be their light. Behold I am coming soon." (Revelations 22:5, ESV). "Blessed is the one who keeps the Words of the prophecy of this book" (Revelations 22:7, ESV).

CHAPTER 54

Understanding Lazarus Expose on the Story of Lazarus

We must allow God to heal us from the pain so deep that it feels like graveclothes binding us deep inside ourselves, hardening over time. We think if we ever start to feel the pain, if we ever start to cry, we would never be able to stop. James Murphy, in the book *Lifted Up between a Pharisee and a Thief*, makes a statement:

> Danger. Do not enter due to risk of explosion. We mistakenly think we will remain forever full of pain, bound in the grave clothes of the past. We must let God call out our wounds, our pain. Just as he called forth Lazarus to come out into the light. Like the tomb of Lazarus, the grave must be opened for there to be a resurrection. Even if it stinks when opened. Sin is the smell of death in God's nostrils, yet

he reaches out to touch us, to embrace us, to fully heal us. (James Murphy)[26]

Only the master surgeon Jesus can cut away the things in our life that bind us like graveclothes. The hurts, disappointments, anger, disillusionment, loss of innocence, abuse—each pain is like a gravecloth that binds our hearts even further. Each binding cloth is something we suffered deep inside. As the father hugged the prodigal son dressed in sin, dressed in rags, and then reclothed him in robes of righteousness, our Father cuts away the sin and pain from our lives and then reclothes us in robes of righteousness. It can be difficult to get through all the sorrow and the pain, but if we believe in Him, He will say to us, "Come forth into the light so I can set you free."

---

[26] *Lifted Up Between a Pharisee and a Thief,* accessed October 7, 2019, https://www.amazon.com/Lifted-Between-Pharisee-Thief-Depth/dp/1500684457.

CHAPTER 55

Watchmen and Gatekeepers

In ancient times, Israel had watchtowers. They are still in use in some hill countries today. The watchmen were used to warn of impending danger. "The Hebrew definition of a watchman is a keeper, a guardian, guard, a shomer. The watchmen had to remain alert to enemy advancement. A watchman always stood vigil. He could see much of what went on in the city: the people, their work, their habits, their lifestyles. The watchmen's role was vital to the townspeople. An understanding of the role of watchmen is vital to a full understanding of the work of God in today's ends-times. "On your walls, O Jerusalem, I have set watchmen; all day and all the night they shall never be silent. You who put the Lord in remembrance, take no rest" (Isaiah 62:6, ESV). "The use of this word communicates that God, like a watchman, is steadfastly keeping guard. He doesn't slumber or sleep, but always keeps a careful watchful eye on Israel and all who 'lift their eyes to the hills,' recognizing that He is the One who preserves, keeps, guards, protects, and watches over His beloved children."[27]

This Bible verse leaves us with a question: Is there a future time it was to be used? Was it also intended for our day? God's message has direct application to the modern-day descendants of the ancient Jews. What does this mean for the work of God today? As this world comes to a prophetic close, we may not have physical watchtowers, but we have spiritual ones. This passage also paints a vivid picture of godly people who are given a unique vision into the world of today. They see the dark clouds gathering on the world's horizon. They mount their posts in prayer and shout out a warning to all who will listen. To the demons, they cry, "Thus far and no farther."

When we ignore our role, we put ourselves and those people we are given charge of in jeopardy.

> For we do not wrestle against flesh and blood, but against the rulers, against the authorities, against the cosmic powers over this present darkness, against the spiritual forces of evil in the heavenly places. Therefore take up the whole armor of God, that you may be able to withstand in the evil day, and having done all, to stand firm. (Ephesians 6:12, ESV)

We are the spiritual watchmen on the wall. A metaphor, sure, but it is very real. It is the spiritual posture that allows the Holy Spirit to use us to intercede and warn others of danger. The Lord has given to each of us the edict. "On your

---

[27] Ibid.

walls, O Jerusalem, I have set watchmen; all the day and all the night they shall never be silent. You who put the Lord in remembrance, take no rest, and give him no rest until he establishes Jerusalem and makes it a praise in the earth" (Isaiah 62:6–7, ESV). Do we sigh and worry about the moral condition of our nation, or do we begin spiritually to see the world through God's eyes? As an intercessor, we stand between God and man, pleading as Moses did, "These are your people, God." We intercede for their very souls.

Our message while warning of danger should also be to intercede to pray that God would raise up godly leaders who would lead His people and would show them the way of salvation. We as watchmen are to stand in vigil like the watchmen of old and show the way forward through the suffering and evil, to be an example both through our lives and our prayers. "Pray without ceasing" (1 Thessalonians 5:17, ESV).

Those who grieve and sigh and cry over sin are called to a unique role they are part of God's elect—intercessors. Fulfilling this role requires love, courage, and perseverance for the people God loves. "First of all, then, I urge that petitions prayers, intercessions and thanksgivings be offered on behalf of all people" (1 Timothy 2:1, AMP). "Therefore, confess your sins to one another and pray for one another, that you may be healed and restored. The heartfelt and persistent prayer of a righteous man can accomplish much. (James 5:16, AMP). The prayer of a righteous man has great power as it is working.

God is a holy God. He loves his people as a father loves his son. But He must respond and bring judgement for sin. Part of our job as watchmen on the wall is to warn of danger. We see it; we must respond. We must warn, and we must pray to turn the tide of evil that seeks to overwhelm. America stands at a crossroads.

For over two hundred years, we have dominated the world. But God warns through the message of the watchman that people cannot continue worshiping false gods of materialism and self. In Jesus's prophecy of the end-times, He urges his disciples three times to watch and pray, to stand at our post, to watch and warn of danger, to pray continually without ceasing. Those watchmen who form their lives around fasting and prayer, walking out their faith in daily living will not be taken unawares. "Listen! Your watchmen lift up their voices, together they shout for joy; for they will see face to face the return of the Lord to Zion" (Isaiah 52:8, AMP). Elijah was a man just like us. He prayed earnestly that it would not rain for three and a half years. Again he prayed, and the heavens gave rain.

The list goes on of godly men who prayed, and God answered. Let us join the prophets of old on the modern-day wall and ask God to touch our generation to be intercessors able to see the danger and give warning.

CHAPTER 56

Two Keys

Two kingdoms, two keys. One is a skeleton key that opens the door to the kingdom of darkness. The other is a gold key that opens the door to the kingdom of light. Both keys are keys to our heart. We have the freewill to choose which key we turn. Sometimes our hearts get confused as darkness beckons with its illusion of fleshly pleasures. Slowly we turn the key to the kingdom of light just enough to hear the King say, "I will never [if you choose the golden key] allow the righteous to be shaken to slip, fall, or fail" (Psalms 55:22, AMP). He then whispers, "I care about you with deepest affection. I will watch over you very carefully" (1 Peter 5:7, AMP).

Satan, the king of darkness, turns the skeleton key slowly, subtly taking away our God-given choice, trying to seal our fate into his kingdom of darkness with addictions and false promises. God, the King of light, tests the heart. "You have tried my heart, you have visited me by night, you have tested me, and you will find nothing; I have proposed that my mouth will not transgress" (Psalms 17:3, ESV). Your light beckons me out of the darkness. Yet as I turn, darkness beckons without words. Using our five senses, he appeals to our human nature. The lies and the promises are subtly veiled. He turns the key tighter and tighter with each step we take toward the dark kingdom.

> The snares of death confronted me. (Psalms 18:5, ESV)

> Streams of ungodliness and torrents of evil terrified me. (Psalms 18:4, AMP)

> In my distress (when I was surrounded by darkness) I called up on the King of light. He heard my voice from his temple. My cry for help came before him into his very ears. (Psalms 18:6, ESV)

> Lord save me Jesus immediately reached out his hand and took hold of me. (Matthew 14:31, ESV)

> He reached from on high, he drew me out of many waters. He rescued me from my strong enemy. (Psalms 18:16–17, ESV)

He rescued me from the kingdom of darkness. As the dawn chases away the darkness. So, the king of light chases away the darkness in our soul.

CHAPTER 57

Walk on Water

One day God said to my problems, "Listen to Me. I got this. Peace I grant you, peace, be still and know I am God. Not just do I speak to the storms of thunder, the spirit of terror but also to your spirit. I calm the waves of frustration, the waves of terror, waves of emotions. Let My Holy Spirit fill you with the calm, soft winds of peace. You are My child. Let go, come walk on water with Me. Take a leap. The net will appear. Step out away from your security, your circumstances. Whatever you hold on to instead of Me, let go. Do not look down. Look at Me. Take My hand. I will catch you. Step out, come walk on water with Me.

> Shortly before dawn Jesus went out to them, walking on the lake. When the disciples saw him walking on the lake, they were terrified. "It's a ghost," they said, and cried out in fear. But Jesus immediately said to them: "Take courage! It is I. Don't be afraid." "Lord, if it's you," Peter replied, "tell me to come to you

on the water." "Come," he said. Then Peter got down out of the boat, walked on the water and came toward Jesus. But when he saw the wind, he was afraid and, beginning to sink, cried out, "Lord, save me!" (Matthew 14:25–30, ESV)

CHAPTER 58

Walking in the Garden

Father, in the late evening, You loved to walk with Adam in the cool of the day, where the breeze blows softly, saying, *It is almost dusk.* "They heard the sound of the Lord God walking in the garden in the cool of the day" (Genesis 3:8, ESV). They hid themselves because of their sin. Father, please come into my heart. Cleanse me, walk with me. I would love to sense Your presence. Come into the garden in my heart. Let it be full of love and gentle whispers from Your heart. Speak to me as You spoke to Samuel. Teach me to listen to Your voice, to recognize Your voice, and respond as Samuel didn't. "The Lord came and stood there, calling as at the other times, 'Samuel! Samuel!' Then Samuel said, 'Speak, for your servant is listening'" (1 Samuel 3:10, NIV). Let me not hide myself from Your holiness because of the lies Satan speaks, that my sins keep You from loving me. I approach your throne covered in rags of sin, but You strip me of my rags of sin, Lord, and replace them with a robe of white. I am covered by the blood of Your Son that I too may walk with You in the garden in the cool of the evening.

CHAPTER 59

Double-Minded

You were created knowing good and evil, having choices. Day by day or by the hour, the Spirit walks within you, but He allows you choices. God does not want cookie-cutter Christians. You have choices, but don't be double-minded. His Spirit as a believer is within you, but you speak with your natural spirit words of slander and anger. Do not be double-minded, speaking words of judgment on one hand and words of love on the other. Some people live two lives. On one side, the Christian walks among other Christians. On the outside at home or work, they speak, out of their natural spirit, hate and discontent. This must not be.

The term *double-minded* comes from the Greek word *dipsuchos*, meaning "a person with two minds or souls."[28] It's interesting that this word appears only in the book of James: "He is a double-minded man, unstable in all his ways" (James 1:8, ESV). "Draw near to God, and he will draw near to you.

---

[28] "What does it mean to be double-minded?" GotQuestions.org, accessed October 5, 2019, https://www.gotquestions.org/double-minded.html.

Cleanse your hands, you sinners, and purify your hearts, you double-minded" (James 4:8, ESV).

> A double-minded person is restless and confused in his thoughts, his actions, and his behavior. Such a person is always in conflict with himself. One torn by such inner conflict can never lean with confidence in God and His gracious promises. Correspondingly, the term unstable is analogous to a drunken man unable to walk a straight line, swaying one way, then another. He has no defined direction and as a result doesn't get anywhere. Such a person is "unstable in all he does."[29]

With our tongue, we bless our Lord; and with it, we also curse people who were made in the image of God. "But no human being can tame the tongue. It is a restless evil, full of deadly poison" (James 3:8, ESV). These things are not to be. Does a spring bring forth from the same opening freshwater and saltwater? Can a fruit tree bear olives or grapevine grow figs? Neither can a salt pond yield freshwater. You were made with choices knowing good and evil. We must not be double-minded, one time choosing one way, the next time choosing another. "Draw near to God, and he will draw near to you. Cleanse your hands, you sinners, and purify your hearts, you double-minded" (James 4:8, ESV).

---

[29] Ibid.

CHAPTER 60

Dark Night of the Soul

In this dark place, may the light of your Spirit pierce the darkness. Becoming a lighthouse, His Spirit dwells within as a beacon of light. A symbol of light invading the darkness. "You are the light of the world. A city set on a hill cannot be hidden" (Matthew 5:14, ESV). I seek to bind the spirits that would disconnect my spirit from Yours. Route the enemy, for I want to worship with you spirit to Spirit. As young Samuel said, "Speak Lord for your servant listens" (1 Samuel 3:10, NIV).

CHAPTER 61

Consuming Fire

Hebrew word for "consuming fire" is *kaesh*. "Then I said, I will not make mention of him nor speak anymore in his name. But his word was in my heart as a burning fire and shut up in my bones, and I was weary with forebearing and I could not stay" (Jeremiah 20:9, NIV). Literally the passage reads, "He was in my heart like a burning fire." Have you ever felt a burning, consuming fire, a kaesh, inside of you?[30] What does the physical fire do? It burns away dried weeds, charred brush. It can also destroy and become larger as it comes flashing through the sins in our lives. Fire can also destroy as it comes flashing into an area of unprotected place. Consuming fire changes us as it comes flashing in all its glory. "For our God is a consuming fire" (Hebrews 12:29, ESV). For the Lord, your God, is a jealous God, intolerant of unfaithfulness in our lives.

Who among us can walk through the consuming fire? In the Old Testament, Shadrach, Meshach, and Abednego

---

[30] Chaim Bentorah, "Hebrew Word Study: A Consuming Fire," accessed October 5, 2019, https://www.chaimbentorah.com/2018/03/hebrew-word-study-a-consuming-fire-2/.

were placed bound in a fiery furnace. The king stood up in awe. He stood as he saw three men walking unbound and a fourth man looking like a son of God walking with them (Daniel 3:24–26, ESV).

Consuming Fire, deliver us into Your throne room. Blow away the chaff. Burn away the dross in my heart in my life. Stir it up, Father, in flames. Grant me, Lord, a passion for Your name.

"I the Lord your God am a consuming fire. I am a jealous impassioned God demanding what is mine" (Deuteronomy 4:24, ESV). Burn away our sins, Lord, in the smelting process. A process where He looks into our lives, skimming off the top, the dross, the things in our life that are not pleasing to Him. Burn them up, Lord. It hurts, Lord, the burning away of the things that are not pleasing to You, but we must submit ourselves to you. The fire of the Spirit like gas is explosive. "Oh Lord, save me and I shall be healed" (Jeremiah 17:14, ESV). We must allow the flames of the Holy Spirit access to the deep things of our heart. "O house of Israel, can I not do with you as this potter has done? declares the Lord. Behold, like the clay on the potter's hand, so are you in my hand, O house of Israel" (Jeremiah 18:6, ESV).

Remember, Father, they are Your people and Your heritage, which You brought out of Egypt to experience the glory of the fiery furnace. For You separated them from among all the people of the earth to be Your heritage. As the consuming fire comes flashing roaring over an area of sin, over an area of unprotected sin of our lives, let us offer to God acceptable consuming worship. Let us offer to God acceptable worship with reverence and awe, for our God is a consuming fire.

Come, Holy Spirit, cleanse me. Let me worship the one true God. I ask for a gentle, quiet heart as I draw close. Quiet my heart as I move into Your throne room. Let the noise of this world slip away as I ascend into your throne. Let me ascend around Your throne in Your high court. Let me worship You, my Savior, as I stand before Your glory, covered in the blood of the cross. Lord, forgive me for taking so lightly Your Son's death as He met Your judgment. Breathe, Holy Spirit of God, fill us anew with your Spirit. Grant us Your fire, a passion for Your name. Let Your fire, Your glory, Father, fall into our lives.

Have Your Way, Lord, a mighty wind rushing in of power. Let Your glory fall. Let Your glory, in all consuming flames, fall. The Israelites were afraid, Lord, of the power of Your Spirit, Your glory, for who among us can dwell within the consuming fire? The flame of Your glory, come breathe within us.

CHAPTER 62

Courts of Heaven

Good morning, Father. My Spirit quickens to the sound of Tour Spirit in the night. The rooster crows, awakening the dawn. I sense Your restlessness, Lord, Your white stallion snorting and impatient, waiting for the order to come bring Your people home, not as servants but as rightful heirs to the throne. Glory and majesty attend You. You are mighty in battle. I ascend this morning to Your court where daily battle plans are made. I cry out with the angels, "Holy, holy, holy is the God of Israel." I come before You with a humble heart. I am ashamed to stand in Your court in my rags of sin and shame. Yet You reach down from Your throne, replacing my garments with robes of righteousness. From Your court, Father, You have commanded Your consecrated ones. You have summoned Your mighty men of prayer to execute Your anger (Isaiah 13:4, ESV). Your great warriors are mustering an army for battle.

CHAPTER 63

Holy Spirit Speaks

My creation, my heart, is broken at the brokenness of My people. My majestic creation, broken, restore them to Me with My Words. Through your teaching, use My anointing, My Holy Spirit. Remember, He is holy, "and do not grieve the Holy Spirit of God, by whom you were sealed for the day of redemption" (Ephesians 4:30, ESV). Stay close. Let Me fill you with the oil of joy. Let your prayers, like incense, rise before Me. Speak to My heart, let the people know how to draw close in fasting and prayer. Daniel, Esther, Job, Paul, even Jesus fasted to draw closer to Jesus. To enter a fast is to enter My presence. "Sackcloth cloth made of black goats' hair, coarse, rough, and thick, used for sacks, and also worn by mourners and as a sign of repentance. It was put upon animals by the people of Nineveh."[31]

Sackcloth is a symbol of giving up the things of the world, the things that are the most dear to you, the things that you hold onto instead of Me. Let it be not a public show

---

[31] "Sackcloth Definition and Meaning," Bible Dictionary, accessed October 5, 2019, https://www.biblestudytools.com/dictionary/sackcloth/.

but between you and Me. It's repentance of a heart crying out. I listen to the cry of My children. I long to draw them under the shadow of My wings. But they rebel and would have none of My protection. My heart longs for them to turn back. Draw them to Me through My Words. I anoint My Words; you must speak My Words. Get them to listen to their Father that they may live. Let Me use you to touch the hearts, to turn them back to me. Without Me, they are battling with plastic swords like children. I laugh in discursion at their childish ways. The enemy laughs. I told Joshua, you cannot stand before your enemy.

CHAPTER 64

Burdens

Don't carry others' burdens. Remember the backpack. Sometimes we carry rocks that aren't ours to carry. They're too heavy for us to bear. That's why I give you balloons in your backpack, full of love, joy, peace, kindness, gentleness, self-control. I see a backpack I'm unable to bear. The heavy backpack carries the rocks of depression, the rock of guilt, the rock of unforgiveness, the rock of pain, the rock of others' burdens, the rock of shame. Christ says my burdens are easy, my burden is light. "Take my yoke upon you, and learn from me, for I am gentle and lowly in heart, and you will find rest for your souls" (Matthew 11:29, ESV).

CHAPTER 65

Creating an Atmosphere

A spiritual atmosphere is climate created by attitude. If you really want to hear from God, you might need to change some of your lifestyle habits. We need to create an atmosphere around us of the Word. "Logos, is the Word of God. There are two primary Greek words that describe Scripture which are translated word in the New Testament. The first, logos, refers principally to the total inspired Word of God and to Jesus, Who is the living Logos."[32]

Rhema, is the Spoken Word. The second primary Greek word that describes Scripture is Rhema, which refers to a word that is spoken and means "an utterance." A Rhema is a verse or portion of Scripture that the Holy Spirit brings to our attention with application to a current situation or need for direction.[33]

---

[32] "What Is a 'Rhema'?" Institute in Basic Life Principles, accessed October 4, 2019, https://iblp.org/questions/what-Rhema.
[33] Ibid.

We need an attitude of honoring God above all others. Are you listening to others instead of seeking God's voice for yourself? In the morning, do you reach for your cell phone before you reach for your Bible? "When God gives a Rhema for us to act upon, He often confirms it by a second Rhema, that 'in the mouth of two or three witnesses shall every word [Rhema] be established'" (2 Corinthians, 13:1).[34]

---

[34] Ibid.

CHAPTER 66

Flood My Heart

Flood my heart with Your presence, Lord
Come, Holy Spirit, come
Let me hear whispers of Your heart
Flood my heart with Your presence
Rise up within me as the path seems dark
Flood my heart with Your presence, Lord

CHAPTER 67

Giftings

It's not our personalities that separate people. It's our giftings. We have different gifts according to God's grace given to us. Each person is unique and different, just as David could not wear Saul's armor for battle. Then Saul clothed David with his armor. David tried in vain to go. Then David said to Saul, "I cannot go with these." We can't wear someone else's giftings. We must be ourselves. Just as we try to wear our parents' Christianity or try to be like someone else we admire. When we fail, we find ourselves going into a tailspin. We try so hard to fit in to the religious groups around us. God does not want cookie-cutter Christians. He's gifted each of us like snowflakes; no two snowflakes are exactly alike, but each shines in their own beauty. Yet coming together, they can make a mighty storm.

God needs each uniqueness, each person, bringing to the body a different style that's uniquely their gifting. "For the gifts and the calling of God are irrevocable" (Romans 11:29, ESV) for special use. We who are many are one body in Christ. "For the body does not consist of one part, but of many" (1 Corinthians 12:14, AMP), united for one cause.

We are parts of one another (dependent on one another). "Be devoted to one another with authentic affection" (Romans 12:10, AMP) (members of one family), giving preference to one another in honor.

CHAPTER 68

A Hole in My Heart

There's a hole in my heart. Sometimes the hole seems so large I can't even breathe. Sometimes the pain is so real I can't bear the grief. So I try on my own to fill the hole with things the world has to offer, trying to find something or someone to fill my heart to ease the pain: relationships. I cling to others, strangling our relationships. My expectations are high. Others cannot bear our pain, so we stuff things in our heart: drugs, alcohol, riches. We seek fame even in religious circles.

We put on a facade where others can't see our pain. We become the life of the party. We dance as fast we can, all the while struggling in our pain. It hurts; we silently cry. We finally find ourselves crying out from deep within our soul, "Lord, save me!" "Jesus immediately reached out his hand and took hold of him, saying to him, 'O you of little faith, why did you doubt?'" (Matthew 14:31, ESV). I offer up my broken heart to You, Lord. Only You can pull me up out of the things the world has to offer. You say in Your Word, "Come unto me you who are weary, and heavy laden. I will give you rest." "The Lord is near to the broken hearted. He saves those who are crushed in Spirit" (Psalms 34:18, ESV).

CHAPTER 69

Helping God

Have you ever felt like you needed to help God, so you mistakenly took matters into your own hands? There have been many times in my life of a lost patience and a wanting to grab hold of the situation to change what was happening. All too often, I've tried to help God and offer my solutions. Inside, I know better, but I still do it. How can I possibly think I know more than God? I can now say, looking back, don't complicate God's promises with your own solutions. Many stories in the Bible tell of men taking things into their own hands. One example would be Sarah's need to control the situation through her handmaiden. So we have the story of Abraham, Ishmael, and Isaac.

In the book of Genesis 16–17, the battle still rages today between the two sons of Abraham. There are many such stories throughout the Bible where man has tried to circumvent God's promises. "A man plans his ways as he journeys through life. But The Lord directs his steps" (Proverbs 16:9, AMP). From experience, no matter how strong, clever, resourceful, or strategic we think we are, we cannot outthink God or try to get ahead of him. Again, how can I think I know more than He does? The problem is, we want what we want now. Our society is geared around an instant answer. We want to microwave instant gratification. We don't want to let things sit and marinate. Each circumstance is another opportunity for God to fulfill his promises. God says, "Wait. Wait for My timing." "Be strong let your heart take courage all who wait for the Lord" (Psalms 31:24, KJV). Then and only then we will see God's glory unfolding. Peter's solution in the garden was to fight. Jesus said to him, "Peter, put your sword away" (John 18:11, NIV). Jesus's solution was to wait by instructing Peter to put away his solution (weapon). There's a bigger picture here.

CHAPTER 70

Journey Home

As I travel on my journey toward home, sometimes the road seems dry and dusty. Sometimes the sandstorms block the light. In my spiritual eye, I see someone walking, casting a shadow in the dust. Suddenly a separate shadow appeared and walked beside him. I then realized the lone figure was me, tired and weary, casting a shadow, walking with a dry and dusty spirit, trying to find my way home.

My heart leaped at the thought that the Carpenter, Jesus, who is the Son of God, walks beside me, guiding my way home. As we walked, He said to my heart, "But the Helper, the Holy Spirit, whom the Father will send in My name, He will teach you all things. And He will help you remember everything that I have told you" (John 14: 26, AMP). In John 14:16–17 (AMP), we read Jesus saying, "And I will ask the Father, and he will give you another Helper, to be with you forever, even the Spirit of truth, whom the world cannot receive, because it neither sees him nor knows him. You know him, for he dwells with you and will be in you." *Helper* ("advocate, counselor, or comforter in other translations") comes from the Greek word *parakletos*. This term referred to a person called alongside another. It includes the idea of one who comforts and assists.[35]

As we walk, Father, fill us with Your Spirit, pour out Your living water (your Holy Spirit) up on us so that Your Spirit may flow through us to others around us. As we walk in this journey, speak to our hearts that we may bring even a cup of living water to Your people, Lord, who also are tired and weary. It is found in the day-to-day living where our life becomes our journey of faith.

---

[35] "What does Paraclete mean? How is the Holy Spirit our...," accessed October 4, 2019, https://www.compellingtruth.org/paraclete-Holy-Spirit.html.

CHAPTER 71

For the joy of the Lord is our strength. Collectively as intercessors, we are a force to be reckoned with—if we come together in love and unity, with the Holy Spirit abiding as a flame in each of us.

CHAPTER 72

Knowing God

Human knowledge, knowing God's Word without the Spirit to guide us, can be like a shallow well. Dirt and debris, scale and murky water abound, making people sick Spiritually with rules and regulations. We need to go deeper beyond the mind of human knowledge to the streams of living water. Deep in the Word is where the living waters are found—beneath all the emotionalism, all the hype, all the traditional practices.

Prayer is what takes us deeper. Real prayer, heartfelt prayer from within our soul, not repeated prayers, not in traditional religious prayers but Spirit-led prayers. Spirit prayers that move us outward. Prayers that move us out of our comfort zone. "For it is not an empty or trivial matter for you; indeed it is your life. By this word you will live long in the land, which you are crossing the Jordan to possess" (Deuteronomy 32:47, AMP). The deep well found in the Word is beneath the scale and murky religions that we see. We need to dig deep in the Word if we are to find the source of this spring of living waters. "For the word of God is living and active, sharper than any two-edged sword, piercing to the division of soul and of spirit, of joints and of marrow, and discerning the thoughts and intentions of the heart" (Hebrews 4:12, ESV). "My inner self thirsts for God, for the living God. When shall I come and behold the face of God?" (Psalms 42:2, AMP).

CHAPTER 73

Morning Fog

This morning, Lord, stand beneath the damp fog. I know by faith that sometimes on our journey home, we don't know which way to go. The fog rolls in, and everything seems obscure. I know by faith, as a result of righteousness, I will have quietness and confident trust in You forever. I know by faith Your Son is above the fog. "Your son, he is like the light of the morning at sunrise" (2 Samuel 23:4, AMP). We stand at a crossroads going which way, Lord? (2 Peter 1:119, ESA). Like a shaft of light shining in the darkness, You go before me.

As I see the bridge through the fog that crosses the dark chasm of my journey, I know by faith You walk beside me. "When you encounter the storm and your foot slips you will only fall to the level of your relationship with God" (Christine Caine).[36] I press on, Father, through the fog. Step by step I follow You across the bridge. "And the effect of righteousness will be peace, and the result of righteousness will be quietness and confidence trust forever" (Isaiah 32:17, AMP). Your

---

[36] Christine Caine, "Unexpected," accessed October 6, 2019, https:// christinecaine.com/unexpected.

Word says the steps of a righteous man are in quietness and confidence trust. "The steps of a man are established by the Lord, when he delights in his way; though he fall, he shall not be cast headlong, for the Lord upholds his hand" (Psalms 37:23, ESV).

CHAPTER 74

Why Worship

Satan rejoices in the face of God at hardened hearts. He comes to steal and destroy. Worship puts a crack in the very heart of those whose heart Satan has hardened or oppressed or filled with pride. Christian worship is a seed planted between the rocks of a hardened spirit so that God's Spirit can begin to grow in a person's heart. Satan has used secular music to steal the hearts of God's people. Satan was a musical angel, a head musical angel. He understands full well the place of worship. That's where his point of pride began. We must worship before we can learn. If we don't, we have head knowledge only. In church, worship comes before theology, opening the hearts of the people to the Word. Worship must come before theology so that our hearts are impacted by the Spirit before our minds are informed so that we also receive heart knowledge.

Worship is the bridge between head knowledge and heart. We must teach people to worship in Spirit and in truth and in Word. True worship teaches submission to authority first to the Word of God, then to the authority over us. King David danced before the Lord in worship, submitting to the spirit of worship. "Then, as the ark of the Lord came into the City of David, Michal, Saul's daughter, looked down from the window above and saw King David leaping and dancing before the Lord; and she felt contempt for him in her heart" (2 Samuel 6:16, AMP).

CHAPTER 75

Oil of the Spirit

The metaphor of oil indicates the continuity of the Holy Spirit's abiding presence and action between Jesus and Christians. Luke through Acts emphasizes a theme that the same Spirit at work in Jesus is now at work in Christians. This theology is concisely restated in the metaphorical statement of anointing. The emphasis is on Jesus as the Anointed One. Using the metaphor of the oil, the oil stands for the intense presence of the power of the Holy Spirit.[37] "Not by might, not by power. But by my Spirit (of whom the oil is a symbol) says the Lord of hosts" (Zechariah 4:6, ESV). "Then Samuel took the horn of oil (and anointed David the Son of Jessie) in the midst of his brothers and the Spirit of the Lord rushed upon David from that time forward" (1 Samuel 16:13, NIV).

To untangle a necklace, drop a little oil into the center of the knot and use a toothpick in the center by lifting

---

[37] "Metaphors Revealing the Holy Spirit, Part 3: Oil as a Metaphor" (March 28, 2016), accessed October 4, 2019, https://www.biola.edu/blogs/good-book-blog/2016/metaphors-revealing-the-holy-spirit-part-3-oil-as-a-metaphor-for-the-holy-spirit.

upward. The chain will slide apart and become untangled. The same thing with our wounds. The Holy Spirit is the oil for our soul. Let the Holy Spirit, as the person is prayed for, begin to apply His oil, soothing oil, pulling our soul wounds gently upward toward the Father. "It is like the precious oil of consecration poured on the head" (Psalms 133:2, ESV). "You have loved righteousness and hated wickedness; therefore God, your God, has anointed you with the oil of gladness (also known the oil spikenard) beyond your companions" (Hebrews 1:9, AMP).

Healing oils such spikenard (also known as nard) is considered one of the more precious of the oils. It is known as the oil of joy. The joy of the Lord is our strength. It relaxes both body and mind—the Rose of Sharon oil, for emotional and physical wounds or cuts, also used for the immune system. Also used to soften and soothe the skin. Frankincense, this an important oil used in religious rites and embalming. It is burned as incense for its sweet smell. The oil of myrrh is an immune booster and is anti-inflammatory. It also was used for healing wounds in ancient Greece. It speeds up healing. The oil of balm of Gilead is highly valued for its aspirin-like quality. It is used for lessening pain, emotional or physical. "Is anyone among you sick? Let him call for the elders of the church and they are to pray over him, anointing his head with oil" (James 5:14, ESV). All these oils are used to symbolize the Holy Spirit upon the person being prayed for, to bring healing, emotional or physical; to draw the anointing of the Spirit of power into their lives.

CHAPTER 76

Living Waters

I love word pictures. Analogies to the natural eye or hearing means one thing but has a whole spiritual context to the spiritual eye. We read in the New Testament in the book of John several times where Jesus says, "I'm the living water." In John 4:14 (ESV), Jesus says, "The water I give you will become in you a spring of water welling up to eternal life." In Aramaic, the word *water* is defined as "from a stream or spring always moving, always flowing." Contrast that with a cistern a dry well—stagnant and unmoving. In the Old Testament in the book of Jeremiah, it said, "God speaks of himself as the fountain of living waters which his people have forsaken for cisterns built by human hands."

In the New Testament, Jesus speaks of the living water as to our spiritual life. "It will be health to your body (your marrow, your nerves, your muscles all your inner parts)" (Proverbs 3:8, AMP). In John chapter 15, Jesus speaks of the living water as a regeneration which is required to be in fellowship with God. In the book of John chapter 4, Jesus tells us how can we obtain this living water—without which our spirits become spiritually emancipated. "The water I will give you will become in you a spring of living welling up to eternal life" (John 4:14, ESV). Let it flow outward onto those around you. We are not to be the well. We are to lead others to Jesus, who is the living water. This living water, the Spirit, can't be kept to ourselves. Otherwise, it will turn into a dry cistern. The first way to obtain the living water is to be in God's Word on a regular basis. Worship on Sundays at church. Have regular fellowship in small groups of friends to feed one another, to touch Jesus, the spring of living water.

Lastly, let it flow outward from you onto others. It can't be kept to yourself because then it becomes stagnant and turns into a dry cistern. The Spirit must always be flowing, always moving. "There is a river whose streams make glad the city of God. The Holy dwelling place of the most high" (Psalms 46:4, NIV). My prayer for each of us would be that we take the living waters of the Holy Spirit and let it flow out of us and use our gifts to touch others so that the Spirit will always stay moving and flowing.

CHAPTER 77

Broken Heart

Father, there is a broken heart. Sew it together with threads of Your love. Weave it together with the colorful threads of Your Spirit, Lord. In ourselves, there needs to be an acknowledgment that there is a heart problem. We must remember there will always be invisible scars, a sign of healing. But they are the result of healing, of opening up our hearts to God and letting Him cleanse it of all the pain, the tears, the sewage of darkness. It will then all flow away like a wound opened up. God's cleansing sometimes is painful, but there would be no need for forgiveness if there was no pain, if there is no need of cleansing.

God desires to put the shattered pieces back together to make a heart whole so that out of our woundedness, we can help other people, so we can breathe without the pain and heaviness of a broken heart. Emotional pain is a sign or a symptom of a need for cleansing. I identify with what Alan Jones says: "My brokenness has known healing because others have reached out to touch me." The story of Christianity is all about the mending of the hearts of the world so that broken hearts can rejoice together in a passion a pilgrimage undertaken for the sake of love.[38]

---

[38] Alan Jones, *Passion for Pilgrimage*, accessed October 7, 2019, https:// www.amazon.com/Passion-Pilgrimage-Alan-Jones/dp/B000XT14LW.

CHAPTER 78

Like a Diamond

I was reading the book *The Shinar Directive*.[39] After much weeping at the state of things, what could look like a losing battle, I went to my Bible and read Nehemiah 8:10–11(ESP): "Do not be grieved for this day is Holy. Be quiet. Do not be grieved, the joy of the Lord is your strength." In my mind's eye, I began to see a beautiful multicolored diamond. A prism of colors shining, flashing harder than flint—a beautiful symbol of love. God is sending his fire a revival, but not of hellfire and brimstone but a firestorm of love using His prayer warriors like a multifaceted diamond showing the fire of his love, uniting Jews and Gentiles with a prism of love and renewal of the colors of His love. A prism of color.

I sense people need to know that the only way out of the darkness is to be overcome by God shining through His people as the fire of love, as the fire in a diamond pure and

---

[39] Dr. Michael Lake, *The Shinar Directive*, accessed October 5, 2019, http://www.armageddonbooks.com/856shinar.html.

holy in their hearts. Then I began to read Ephesians 2:14–16 (ESV), talking about Jews and Gentiles:

> For he himself is our peace, who is made us both one and has broken down in his flesh the dividing wall of hostility. By abolishing the commandments expressed in ordinances, that he might create in himself one new man in place of the two so making peace, and reconciling us both to God in one body through the cross killing the hostility. He came and preached peace to those who are far off and peace to those who are near. In him we are being built together. A dwelling place for God by his Spirit.

God is reuniting the Jews and the Gentiles in these last days. As a diamond flashes fire in beauty, so His love flashes and unites the hearts of the Jews and Gentiles alike.

CHAPTER 79

The Ways of God in Our Time

Behold, the former things have come to pass, and new things I now declare; before they spring forth I tell you of them. (Isaiah 42:9, ESV)

Who among you will give ear to this, will attend and listen for the time to come? (Isaiah 42:23, ESV)

Remember not the former things, nor consider the things of old. (Isaiah 43:18, ESV)

Behold I am doing a new thing now it springs forth do you not perceive it? (Isaiah 49:19, ESV)

Incline your ear, and come to me; hear,
that your soul may live. (Isaiah 55:3,
ESV)

Each new move of God is known for its uniqueness.
What is the form God will take in our day? We know how He
moved in the past, but how will He appear in our time these
last days? Are there ways we have not seen or experienced?
The question is, will we accept the new move of God, or will
we judge it? God wants to open our eyes spiritually so we can
see Him in a new way. My question is, how do we access this
new move of God? (Barbie Breathitt).[40]

CHAPTER 80

Jesus — White Stallion

I saw Jesus standing in the stirrups on a white stallion waving a flag over the valley of decision—weeping, waiting for a word from His Father when He could take His rightful place. The voice was the lion of Jordan. Your Savior is but a hill away. The flag He is waving in victory has a bloodstained cross on it.

CHAPTER 81

Seeking Peace

As the silence of this day descends into my heart, as I seek out your heart after the chaos of the day, Your peace descends upon my heart. Father, Your world that You created is in chaos, thrown there by the king of darkness, held down by chains of darkness. Some don't even know You exist. Their spiritual eyes and ears are blinded by the God of this world. Some sit in churches, but their hearts are far from You. Some try to replace you with gods of their own making. Their hearts are hardened against the truth, not wanting to acknowledge that You alone are the one true God.

To the wicked, God says, "Now consider this, you who forget God. What right do you have to recite My statutes? Or to take My covenant upon your lips? (communion). For you hate Instruction and discipline. You disregard my Words. You give your mouth to evil" (Psalms 50:16, AMP). "Your tongue frames deceit, you sit and speak against your brother" (Psalms 50:19, AMP). "But now consider this; He who offers a sacrifice of praise and thanksgiving honors me; him who follows the way I show him. I shall show him the way of salvation" (Psalms 50:23, AMP).

CHAPTER 82

Seeking God's Will

It's easy to start seeking God's direction more than just seeking to know the Father's heart. When frustration comes about wanting to know God's will in your life, find some time to just sit before God in worship and quietness. We must get to know His heart rather than just wanting to get something from Him. Don't bypass the relationship because you would rather have your questions answered. Refocus on God. Sit quietly and worship. God will begin to open doors in His will for your life.

Learn the names of God. God will begin to show Himself and His mighty power through His names. "He made known his ways to Moses, his acts to the people of Israel" (Psalms 103:7, ESV). "Now therefore, if I have found favor in your sight, please show me your ways, that I may know you in order to find favor in your sight. Consider too that this nation is your people" (Exodus 33:13, ESV). Moses wanted something more. Now, if indeed I have found favor with you, please teach me Your ways, and I will know You.

The names of God in the Old Testament: El Shaddai (Lord God Almighty), El Elyon (the Most High God),

Adonai (Lord, Master), Yahweh (Lord, Jehovah), Jehovah Nissi (the Lord My Banner), Jehovah-Raah (the Lord My Shepherd), Jehovah Rapha (the Lord That Heals), Jehovah Shammah (the Lord Is There), Jehovah Tsidkenu (the Lord Our Righteousness), Jehovah Mekoddishkem (the Lord Who Sanctifies You), El Olam (the Everlasting God), Elohim (God), Qanna (Jealous), Jehovah Jireh (the Lord Will Provide), Jehovah Shalom (the Lord Is Peace), Jehovah Sabaoth (the Lord of Hosts).

CHAPTER 83

Eagles' Wings

Father, I rise this morning on eagles' wings above the storms of life. I enter Your presence. You hide me on eagles' wings. As the parent eagle flies beneath the babies to catch them as they are learning to fly, Your Spirit flies under us to lift us up to draw us closer to Your ways, to catch us if we fall in life's storms. Lord, we get tired, but You are there to bear us up on eagles' wings to yourself. "You have seen what I did to the Egyptians, and how I carried you on the wings of eagles and brought you to Myself" (Exodus 19:4, ESA). I bore us up on eagles' wings to give you rest above the storms of life. Eagles with their tail feathers and pinions used as a rudder, they can fly at peace, flying at tent thousand feet above the storm, resting on thermal winds to support them.

As we go through the storms of our lives with our Spirit rising up to meet Your Spirit acting as a rudder. With Your Spirit beneath us, we rise at peace with You with healing in Your wings. You are the wind beneath our wings.

CHAPTER 84

A Broken Heart

Two kings battle for our soul. The king of darkness, Satan, and the King of light, God. Darkness beacons with its sense of worldly independence, its sense of pleasures unlimited. We turn our backs on the light. After all, what does the light have to offer? Obedience, rules. "For you say, I am rich, I have prospered, and I need nothing, not realizing that you are wretched, pitiable, poor, blind, and naked" (Revelations 3:17, ESV). Satan whispers to your mind, "No one loves you." As we turn toward the darkness, the king of darkness inserts daily a skeleton key deeper and deeper in our soul, shutting out the light into our hearts, claiming victory. Satan laughs in the face of God, the King of light. "How can you redeem her? How can you buy her back? For you are a God of holiness, and she is covered with sin and shame. You can't even look upon her. One more twist of the key, and she's mine. Her spirit begins to die within her. Spiritual death—the ultimate betrayal."

A broken heart worn down by the ravages of time, broken and bruised. You shed a tear; your childlike heart is broken. We ask, do You see our tears shed in darkness, sometimes in silence? You who created us, the King of light, longs to wipe away each tear. We shed tears; we weep as He weeps. He longs to redeem us, to buy us back from slavery from the king of darkness. Satan demands a sacrifice, the ultimate sacrifice of blood: the King's Son. The king of darkness will settle for nothing less. The King of light weeps. He says to the king of darkness, "Take note, I will make those of the synagogue of Satan, who say that they are Jews and are not, but lie, I will make them come and bow down at your feet and make them know that I have loved you" (Revelations 3:9, AMP). Come and bow down at my feet and make known to them without any doubt that I have loved them.

CHAPTER 85

Wind of the Kite

We can compare working for God without the wind of the Spirit to a little boy flying a kite on a windless day. He runs furiously up and down the sidewalk, pulling his lifeless kite behind him. As long as he runs, the kite seems to fly. The moment he relaxes, the kite falls to the ground. His problem? The wind isn't blowing. In the church, if we're not careful, we replace the blowing wind of the Holy Spirit with endless programs, seminars, classes, committee meetings, planning sessions. We often try to carry the church by our own human efforts. What the church desperately needs is a new wind of the spirit. When the Holy Spirit does come, we must not quit our programs or seminars. The difference is, the Spirit fills our work and lifts it up far beyond the world of human expectations and limitations, doing "immeasurably more than all we ask or imagine."

CHAPTER 86

Jeremiah 29:4—13

Israel was taking into exile into Babylon in 587 BC. Exile is to be banished, expelled, or to be driven off. If you are exiled from a place, you must leave and not return. Such punishment is called exile.[41]

> For thus says the Lord: When seventy years are completed for Babylon, I will visit you, and I will fulfill to you my promise and bring you back to this place. For I know the plans I have for you, declares the Lord, plans for welfare and not for evil, to give you a future and a hope. Then you will call upon me and come and pray to me, and I will hear you. (Jeremiah 29:10–12, ESV)

As long as the people thought they might be going home at any time, it made no sense to engage in committed

---

[41] "Exile—Dictionary Definition," Vocabulary.com, accessed October 6, 2019, https://www.vocabulary.com/dictionary/exile.

faithful work in Babylon. If there is a good chance that they would soon get back all that they had lost, there is no need to develop a life of richness, texture, and depth where they were. They could be casual and irresponsible in their relationships and in their religion. They weren't going to see these people much longer anyhow.

The people, glad for a religious reason to be lazy, live hand to mouth, irresponsible in their relationships and in their religion and in politics, indifferent to the reality of their actual lives (Jeremiah 29:4, ESV), but Jeremiah the prophet had a message, a letter, to the exiles of Israel from God. This is the message from God of the angel armies, Israel's God: "To all the exiles., build houses and make yourself at home. Marry and have children. Work for the country's welfare. Pray for the Babylonians well-being" (Jeremiah 29:5, ESV). Pray to the Lord on its behalf, for in the Babylonians' peace, you will find peace there.

What do we do about the rapture, about one day going home to heaven? We question, why do I have to get involved? After all, I'm going home to heaven. After all, this is not my home. I'm just an alien here. Why do I need to get committed? I'm leaving soon. My real home is in heaven. What do these heathens have to do with me? I can't relate. My relationships don't matter. I can be irresponsible in my relationships, in my commitments, in my religion. Why do I need to help the poor, the widow.? After all, I'm not going to see them much longer anyhow. Put up fences, put up gates. Keep those people out. Why bother? I'll go to church on Sundays to keep my salvation. But to get involved, to be committed, to help the church with its programs that help the homeless, the alcoholic, the divorcee, the orphan? To raise the next-generation kids as godly children? Why bother? I'm going home soon. You are not camping.

"This is your home no matter how temporary" (Eugene Peterson).[42] Go to work, get involved in a church, school, community, relationships. Make a difference in politics. Help change those laws and rules that make people irresponsible and ungodly. No matter who these people are, be Jesus's hands, His feet, His voice. Help the orphan, the widow, the homeless, the downtrodden. Jesus also was here on a temporary basis. But His example was to get involved, to give people hope, to lead people to the streams of living water. Our goal should be to bring as many of them as believers on the journey home with us. Your task as a person of faith is to develop trust, conversation, love, understanding. "The aim of a person of faith should not be to live as comfortable as possible. But to live as deeply and thoroughly as possible" (Eugene Peterson).[43]

---

[42] Eugene H. Peterson, *Run with the Horses*, R3 Alliance, accessed October 7, 2019, http://r3alliance.com/2017/02/run-with-the-horses-by-eugene-h-peterson/.

[43] Ibid.

CHAPTER 87

Deceitfulness

"But exhort one another every day, as long as it is called "today," that none of you may be hardened by the deceitfulness of sin" (Hebrews 3:13, ESV). When we do something we know is wrong, when we sin against someone else intentionally or accidentally, when we sin—we avoid God. We hide from God the things we have done. We can name many men in the Bible who were deceitful. But if we do, are we trying to justify our own deceit? The Hebrew meaning for *deceit* is "deception, dishonesty, and treachery."[44] The Bible tells us the heart is deceitful above all things. In the book of Jeremiah, God says, "I the Lord search the heart and test the mind" (Jeremiah 17:10, ESV). He searches us to see why we do what we do. What is your heart speaking, your conscience? We have King David, we have King Saul, we have Jacob, who was later to become Israel, the leader of Israel— all deceitful men, all dishonest with deception and treachery. The Spirit is willing, but the flesh is weak. "For when he

---

[44] "What is another word for deceit?," WordHippo, accessed October 6, 2019, https://www.wordhippo.com/what-is/another-word-for/deceit.html.

received honor and glory from God the Father, and the voice was borne to him by the Majestic Glory, "This is my beloved Son, with whom I am well pleased" (2 Peter 1:17, ESV). Take care you're not carried away with lawlessness and error, lest you to lose your own stability.

Satan plays with our heads with dark talons at the back of our mind. He grabs us, placing his thoughts in our hearts. He reminds us of what we did to cause us shame and guilt Hebrews 3:8 (AMP) says, "Today if you hear God's voice do not harden your heart as they did in their rebellion." If God is pointing his Spirit at something in your life, do not pull away. Do not despise the discipline of the Lord. King David said, "I have been disciplined by the Lord but I surely did not die." Satan would have you think because of what you did, God will not love you or forgive you. You will carry guilt and shame like sharp talons in your heart. But the love of the Father always prevails.

As the prodigal son who lived a life of sin and degradation of guilt and shame, he came home to the father with his head down, full of shame and guilt. The father welcomed him with open arms, washing him and dressing him in robes of righteousness, *forgiving* him. Come home today to the Father. Bring your sin, your guilt, your shame to the Father, who loves you, who forgives you. Do not harden your heart. Hear His voice saying, "Come home. All is forgiven. You are now a son, and you have learned obedience through what you suffered."

CHAPTER 88

Smelting Process

Something You showed me yesterday, Father—you cannot have olive oil without the intense pressure that the olive must go through to produce the oil. Father, in Your Word, You're constantly refining us as silver and gold. "For you, O God, have tested us; you have tried us as silver is tried" (Psalms 66:10, ESV). This smelting process is painful and hard. You take the hard things in our lives and put them into the smelting process into the vat of the Holy Spirit.

The silversmith (the Holy Spirit) then stirs the vat (our lives). Our sins rise to the surface as scum to a silversmith. The dross in our lives, the things in our life that are not pleasing to God, are slowly removed. The silversmith repeats this process often. As things rise to the surface that are not honoring to Him, He continually skims them away through the smelting or repentance process until God, the Silversmith, sees His reflection in the silver or gold of our lives.

CHAPTER 89

River of Life

Today after much rain in the natural, in my mind's eye, I saw a raging river. I saw people's hearts as rocks in the river. Jagged, rough, hardened hearts. The hearts were being tumbled around and around in the raging current of the river of life, where the continuous buffeting by life changes the structure of the rocks. The Spirit smooths away the jagged life-worn edges of our hearts. He wears away the outward roughness that we stab other people with. As we are tumbled in the river of life—physical ailments, financial troubles, marital troubles, family problems, and mental illness—God uses the rock tumbler of life to begin to smooth away our roughness, to polish our hearts. As we are buffeted against people and circumstances, we begin to lose our roughness. As we begin to live in the Word, as we begin to let the Spirit quiet our hearts, the rock tumbler begins to slow down to move us into a slower current in the river of life.

The river of life flows from the source, which is the Word. As you find yourself in the Word, not fighting against the current, you'll find a quiet place in your heart, a place of peace. Go down to Shiloh (a sacred place where the tabernacle of the Lord rested for three hundred years). The Jewish people went there to connect with God. That is why when you hear, "Go down to Shiloh," go to that place inside you where you can now connect with the Spirit of God. There you will find peace and rest for your soul.

"There is a river whose streams make glad the city of God, the holy habitation of the Most High" (Psalms 46:4, ESV). There you will find blessings and words to encourage, to teach, touching hearts, softening hard, wounded hearts with sometimes just a gentle blowing touch, sometimes strength beyond your imagination. There is strength in gentleness, for the Word works quietly, invisibly to turn rebellious wounded hearts once again to the Father. God tumbles us out of the rough raging river of life into a gentle bubbling stream called living waters, polishing us into beautifully seasoned hearts where people can see His beauty.

CHAPTER 90

Sabbath Day

The sun has risen to welcome a new day. As it rises, we welcome also Your Spirit as it rises as an eagle on the dawn of the morning wind. May our prayers rise up like incense before You. This day is dedicated to Your Sabbath, Your holy day.

CHAPTER 91

Storm Warnings

Storm clouds gather on the horizon with lighting flashing, thunder rumbling in the distance. In the spiritual world, there are also clouds rumbling. In our spirits, we sense the coming storm between light and darkness. "You who are still worshiping on the mountain top raise your hands in praise and worship. I call you as watchmen on the wall to awaken my people with the sound of the shofar (ram's horn). Wake yourself, wake yourself, stand up, O Jerusalem, you who have drunk from the hand of the LORD the cup of his wrath, who have drunk to the dregs the bowl, the cup of staggering" (Isaiah 51:17, ESV)

As the storm begins to gather strength in the spiritual, we read in Your Word that You are mustering together an army of Jews and Gentiles alike bound in the unity of the Spirit. You are building a spiritual wall. "I appointed watchmen over you and said, 'Listen to the sound of the trumpet!' But you said, 'We will not listen'" (Jeremiah 6:17, NIV).

CHAPTER 92

Light into Darkness

I have not called you out of the darkness to curse the darkness. But I have called you to be a light into the darkness so there's a way that people can see beyond the absolute darkness of their life. Let your light like a beacon in a stormy place or as the lights of a runway for a plane. We are to be that light, however small we feel or how inadequately feel. It's not feelings that matter; it's forgiveness and love from the heart.

CHAPTER 93

Rocks Backpack

"Come to me, all who labor and are heavy laden, and I will give you rest. Take my yoke upon you, and learn from me, for I am gentle and lowly in heart, and you will find rest for your souls. For my yoke is easy, and my burden is light" (Matthew 11:28–30, ESV). Most of us in life use a backpack. We stuff it with many things; we overstuff it to the point we can't carry it. What about spiritually? What do we carry spiritually in our backpacks? Sometimes we carry rocks that aren't ours to carry, even when they're too heavy for us to bear. Rocks could be all the things in our lives that keep us from God: jealousy, hatred, or a past full of woundedness, anger, relationships gone bad, idols in our life that we worship more than God. Sometimes we do come to church. We lay our burdens or backpacks at the cross the rocks. The burden of the rocks bows us down with oppression.

The problem is sometimes we pick up our backpack from the cross and take it home with us. We stumble out of the church as oppressed as when we went in. At the cross, there's a new backpack. That backpack is full of balloons of the Holy Spirit, light and airy. The balloons are filled with the

Spirit. Each balloon is filled with love joy, peace, goodness, gentleness, and self-control. Again. "Come to me, all who labor and are heavy laden, and I will give you rest" (Matthew 11:28, ESV). Heavy laden with the rocks of depression, the rock of guilt, the rock of unforgiveness, the rocks of past pain, the rocks of others burdens. "For each will have to carry his own load" (Galatians 6:5, ESV).

Satan will defuse our power by simply downplaying in our minds the true position of us in Christ. "There's a saying going around. Sometimes in life when things get hard I remember whose daughter I am and straighten my crown. For I am a child of the King."

CHAPTER 94

Tangled Yarn

Our lives sometimes resemble a tangled, knotted ball of yarn—each knot being something, a situation, maybe a relationship in our lives that leave us feeling entangled, stuck in a place of pain and difficulty. It hurts, especially when the ball starts to unravel, when our past begins to catch up with our present. "I am weary with my moaning; every night I flood my bed with my tears. I wasted away because of my grief" (Psalms 6:6, ESV).

God asks us to let Him slowly begin to unravel the yarn His way, pulling on the yarn piece by piece, little by little. We must be careful not to rush the process. Some knots have lasted for years. Some tangles and knots have lasted so long we think that's just the way things are. Some people can't even remember the reason the knots, the tangles, are even there in the first place. Taking each memory, each circumstance, that leads to the tangle, we begin to see a ball of hurts, frustrations, broken promises, pain, abuse, lies, and deceit.

Yet our God sees a masterpiece that can be made from the same tangled ball of yarn that we feel can't be used for anything and needs to be thrown out. Once we let him begin to untangle the yarn, He pulls slowly. He gently pulls and tugs with the greatest love, pointing out one more tangle, one more knot. When all is said and done, the most beautiful things can be made from letting God untangle our lives. After all, He knows us. He created us. "I will give thanks with my whole heart I will recount all your wonderful deeds. I will be glad and exult in you; I will sing praises to your name oh most high" (Psalms 9:12, ESV).

CHAPTER 95

Threads of Love

Father, there is a broken heart. Help me sew it together with threads of Your love, to weave it together with the colorful threads of Your Spirit, Lord. In ourselves, there needs to be an acknowledgment that there is a heart problem. We must remember there will always be invisible scars, a sign of healing. But they are the result of healing, of opening up the heart to God and letting Him cleanse it off all the pain, the tears, the sewage of darkness. It will then all flow away like a wound opened up. God's cleansing sometimes is painful. But there would be no need for forgiveness if there was no pain. No need of cleansing. God desires to put the broken, shattered pieces back together to make a heart whole so that out of our woundedness, we can help other people, so they can breathe without the pain and heaviness of a broken heart. Emotional pain is a sign or a symptom of a need for cleansing. I identify with what Alan Jones in his book *Passion for Pilgrimage* says: "My brokenness has known healing because others have reached out to touch me. The story of Christianity is all about the mending of the hearts of the world so that broken hearts can rejoice together in a passion a pilgrimage undertaken for the sake of God's love."[45]

[45] Alan Jones, *Passion for Pilgrimage: Notes for the Journey Home*, accessed October 7, 2019. https://books.google.com/books/about/Passion_for_Pilgrimage.html?id=j69EAwAAQBAJ.

CHAPTER 96

Finding God

Where can I find You, Lord? I go into the deep; You are not there. I enter the heavens; I could not find You. Then in my heart, I sense Your presence. I find Your Spirit residing inside me. "You know him, for he dwells with you and will be in you" (John 14:17, ESV). "'Peace be with you. As the Father has sent me, even so I am sending you.' And when he had said this, he breathed on them and said to them, 'Receive the Holy Spirit'" (John 20:21–22, ESV). Remind me daily that Your Spirit resides within me. "But from there you will seek the Lord your God and you will find him, if you search after him with all your heart and with all your soul" (Deuteronomy 4:29, ESV).

Teach me to walk according to Your Word in a Spirit of holiness. Anoint your Words, Lord, that others may understand, that they may experience Your presence. Let my heart become one with Your heart, two hearts beating as one. I listen for Your voice in the early dawn, before the day awakens. Create in me clean hands and a pure heart so that through Your Spirit, Lord, I may enter Your presence.

CHAPTER 97

The Call of God

Sometimes what God is asking of us can be intimidating, unusual, scary. What is God asking you to do that seems bigger, beyond what you are incapable in your own self? There are many men in the Bible that felt inadequate and unsure about the call of God. "I call heaven and earth today to witness against you that I've set before you life and death. Blessings and curses. Choose life that you and your offspring may live. love the Lord your God. Obey his voice holding fast to him, for he is your life and ancient of days" (Deuteronomy 30:19, ESV).

We don't feel adequate as we read about these mighty men in the Bible. They all had the same mind-set. They had a lack of pride, a definite humility, and a dependence on God. Their dependence on God was so strong that they obeyed his call. God called Abram out of the darkness of his culture into the light of His promise. Abram didn't question when God told him to leave his land and his people. When the call of God came, he obeyed. We read about King David. King David was the least in his father's house, yet he became the most powerful king because of his heart. The Bible says that "God called him a man after my own heart because of his praise and worship for me" (Judges 6:15, ESV). Gideon's response, when he heard the call, was, "I am the least, the weakest in Manasseh. And I am the least in my father's house." After he obeyed Gideon broke down many altars of Bale, including one his father had built. He obeyed the call. Moses said, "I can't, O Lord, I have a speech impediment," yet he became the friend of God and a great leader of God's people. He obeyed the call. The prophet Ezekiel said, "I am but a child," yet he listened and obeyed the call. He became a great prophet. God replied, "This commandment I give you today is not so hard for it is not in heaven that you should ascend that many will hear and do it. My Word is very near you. It is in you. In your mouth and in your heart so that you can do it. I am in your heart so that you can do it" (Deuteronomy 30:11–12, ESV). Saul hid behind the baggage; they brought him out and anointed him. He obeyed the prophet Samuel and became king.

We see that all these men had one thing in common. They loved God and obeyed Him. They all had a dependence on God. "It is the Lord who goes before us. He will be with us he will not leave us or forsake us. Do not fear" (Deuteronomy 30:14, ESV). God calls us out into deeper waters. Out where the only thing we can do is depend on Him. Sometimes all we can do is be like Peter, who asked, "Lord, is it You? Do You want me to do this? Do You want me to walk on water? Where are You leading me?" God is asking you to step out of the boat and take His hand. He's there to catch you, as He did Peter.

CHAPTER 98

Warfare and Worship

I come into your throne room. I drop my crown that the world would give me at Your feet and pick up Your crown of thorns that Your love for me cost You. War costs. War is a battle. A real battle fought between two opposing forces. This battle is fought on the spiritual level between God and Satan. It cost You your life. What will it cost me? As I go to war, I count the costs. What will I give up to follow You into battle? Which side of the cross am I on? You hung that day between two thieves. One said, "If you really are the son of God, get us down from here." In other words, "What can you do for me? I seek Your hand." The other thief said, "You truly are the Son of God. Remember me when You come into Your kingdom." In other words, "I seek Your bloodstained face. I follow You." Peter was so humbled to be crucified like Jesus he asked to be crucified upside down because he didn't feel worthy to be crucified like Christ. What is your Christianity in this battle costing you?

Father, make us known to the spirit world, ready to go in and conquer the enemy spiritually. With boots on (shod with the Gospel of peace), we hit the ground running—with your sword (your Word) in our hands. In all circumstances of war, we take up the shield of faith to extinguish the darts of the enemy, our hearts and minds at all times praying in the spirit, as You did with Joshua in the Old Testament when You called him into battle. You send the captain of the army of hosts with us to reveal the strategic battle plans of the enemy.

God gives us a strategic battle plan: worship and warfare. Worship words do not disappear into nothingness. They have no geographical limitations. Worship words have power, presence, and prophetic implications. They sound like the shofar (the ram's horn) does in the spirit realm as we do worship warfare.

While the words *worship* and *warfare* are familiar, they produce in us opposing emotions. Every war has a cause or purpose. Napoleon marched in quest of territory. The United States attacked Iraq to protect oil interest. But a far greater war is being fought—in the spiritual dimension, fought on earth and in the heavenlies.

Warring involves taking a stand, overcoming a threat, conquering an enemy. The typical thought process does not include worship in the battle plan. Our thinking needs to change. God in His Word calls us to ascend in worship to His throne room, be clothed in His authority, and then descend in war. Will the enemy recognize our anointing after we've been in God's presence? The answer is a resounding yes.

Whom does God use to go to war? God loves common people. That's why He made so many of us. He is calling as He did in the New Testament *everyday people*. Carpenters, computer programmers, bus drivers, farmers—anyone who will listen to his call. "Come, follow Me." It is everyday people who fill the ranks of God's army. He calls us out as the physical army does from our everyday lives to go to war. Spiritual war. The question God asked Adam in Genesis is chilling: Where are you? I'm sure God is asking many of us this same question: Where are you? This is a time for worship and war. Ascend, go up in worship, descend, come down to war. What a paradox.

We would rather if the truth be known, sit on the mountaintop, and just worship. But when you add intercession to worship, we begin to see God's heart for the things a little further down the mountain. We see Him wanting to touch the valley and those who are in it: the lost, the wounded, those held in all sorts of bondage. He longs to touch the government, the economic system. His heart wants to save the unborn child. All of this entails war. Spiritual war. We worship so that we may go to war with Him.

History makes us see that Satan convinces us that as long as we give up what is ours, we will not have to face war. If we give up our rights, war will be averted. If we give our children as slaves to him, war can be averted. The question is, how far are we willing to go? We have given up prayer in schools. We have given up the rights of the unborn. We have allowed a small minority to say what is acceptable in our society, all in the name of war. We have not been vigilant. And much has been lost by the casualties of us not going to war. God wants His people back. We have felt His heart in intercession; we have heard His heart's desires in prophetic words. It's time to go out and stand up to the thief, come what may. "It's time for war." Which side are you on?

CHAPTER 99

Watchmen on the Wall

In the book of Hebrews, the word for "intercession" is *paga*, "meaning to meet." We are not just a prayer, a person's praise, or something a person does. We can only do it through the Spirit leading us, guiding us. They define intercession as "carrying a spiritual burden for an individual or situation it includes cities, states and nations. Intercession entails praying until God's plan is fulfilled."[46]

When God calls you to intercession, it is usually in a secluded place with little or no credit that will be seen. The giant sequoia redwoods with trunks over 350 feet high have a root system that are only six to eight feet deep. The thing that keeps the redwoods stable and standing tall is that the root systems are so intertwined for hundreds of feet in all directions with the roots of other redwoods—so intertwined that you cannot even dig through it. Walking up on it is like walking on rocks. So interconnected that the hidden-away root system supports the entire redwood tree. As intercessors,

---

[46] *Lifted Up Between a Pharisee & a Thief: An In-Depth Look at...*, accessed October 7, 2019, https://www.amazon.com/Lifted-Between-Pharisee-Thief-Depth/dp/1500684457.

we must sometimes be hidden away, hidden from the eye of the world. But we are the support system of the Christian church, the special ops team that goes in before the physical battle.

Intercession creates a meeting. Intercessors must meet with God daily. They also must confront the powers of darkness from their place as watchmen on the wall. No one is born a prayer hero. We are shaped, molded, and refined on the practice field of life just like any other pursuits in life sports, art, music. Our chosen professions need refining, so it is in our prayer life. We need to practice, practice, practice, and do much listening to those in authority over us as the spirit leads.

Prayer is a partnership of the child of God working together with God toward His redemptive purposes on earth. Our intercessory prayers will always and only be an extension of His intercessory work. This is crucial to remember. In Deuteronomy, Moses interceded for the Israelites: "For I was afraid of the anger and hot displeasure that the Lord had against you, he was ready to destroy you. But the Lord listened to me at that time also, I lay prostrate before the Lord 40 days and 40 nights. I ate neither bread and or drink water because of all the sin you had committed. Doing what was evil in the sight of the Lord to provoke Him to anger" (Deuteronomy 9:18). I prayed to the Lord, "Oh, Lord God, do not destroy Your people and Your heritage, whom You have redeemed through Your greatness."

Understanding why we do something can be a great motivating force. Moses loved the Israelites, his people, and he knew God loved them. He knew God had chosen them. He interceded for them; he stood between them and God, just as Christ now stands between us and God as our mediator, *paga*. Our meeting with God is to make another meeting a reconciliation. We meet with Him asking Him to meet with someone else. We become the go-between, just as Jesus is our advocate between us and the Father. Through the Holy Spirit, we become an advocate for other people. We intercede for them as Moses did for the Israelites. "For there is one God and there is one mediator between God and man Jesus Christ" (1 Timothy 2:5). Asking in His name, praying in His name, means He is interceding for us so that God will hear our prayers. Christ is our righteousness.

CPSIA information can be obtained
at www.ICGtesting.com
Printed in the USA
FSHW011320030220
66773FS